BOROUGH OF TWICKENHAM I

OCCASIONAL PAPER No. 4

YORK HOUSE, TWICKENHAM

by

T.H.R. CASHMORE

May 1990

Twitnam, where Hyde, majestic sage,
Retir'd from folly's frantic stage,
While his vast soul was hung on tenters,
To mend the world and vex dissenters . . .

(Horace Walpole, The Parish Register
of Twickenham, 1758)

ISBN 0 903341 51 4

CONTENTS

ILLUSTRATIONS AND MAPS

The cover illustration is a detail from Edward Ironside's
"A View of Twickenham" – 1786

PREFACE

When Jane Austen, then aged 16, wrote a brief History of England, she attributed it to a partial prejudiced and ignorant historian. Now I am compelled to admit that this brief History of York House is also a partial one in the sense of things omitted either through ignorance or lack of expertise. I have avoided any detailed examination of the interior or its furnishings although there is no lack of evidence from the 1870s onwards, not least in the form of photographs dating back to the 1890s. Furthermore, I have avoided close examination of the architectural history of the House since the evidence is sometimes lacking and often contradictory. I have, it is true, hazarded a personal opinion as to the dating of the central core of the house, hiding behind the fact that even Niklaus Pevsner could date the house as circa 1700 in the first edition of his Middlesex volume of *The Buildings of England* (1951), yet thirty years later amend this date to the 1650s. But for those of you who want something more tangible, an annexe has been prepared on the architectural history of the building and on some of the unanswered problems. With the annexe there is a chronology and an outline plan of the ground floor of York House. The annexe is the work of Anthony Beckles Willson who is an architect, a sculptor, and an historian. He has examined the house in some detail before preparing this annexe. We owe him a debt of gratitude.

It is to be hoped that during the present work of renovation and restoration, the opportunity will be seized to carry out a close examination of the bones — or at least the core — of the old house, so that experts can give us a more certain guidance as to dating. Until that "autopsy" is complete, it will not be possible to offer more conclusive findings.

T.H.R.C.
March 1990.

Fig. 1.   A View of Twickenham by Edward Ironside 1786

Fig. 2. View of the front of York House
by courtesy of Donald W. Insall and Associates Limited

Fig. 3.   View of the rear of York House from the Gardens

Fig. 4. Restored Statuary Group in York House Gardens, 1989

YORK HOUSE, TWICKENHAM

by T.H.R. Cashmore

PROLOGUE

Tradition and legend have it that York House, Twickenham was so called after James, Duke of York (subsequently James II) and that his daughters Mary and Anne (subsequently Queen Mary II and Queen Anne) had been nursed as babes in the House.* Tradition goes further and says that Anne was born in York House and at one time a room, known as "Queen Anne's Chamber" commemorated that event. The truth is more mundane. From the fourteenth to the sixteenth centuries a family called York or Yorke owned land in Twickenham to which they added over the years so that in time their holdings became separated from the older and larger Manor of Isleworth. A new manor was formed with its own manor court, usually called the Manor of Twickenham, but also referred to, as late as the 19th Century, as "York Manor" or even "Yorkhold". This name persisted long after the York family had left Twickenham. As for Queen Anne, although she was not born in York House, and probably never visited it, she did spend the summer of 1694 with her son, the sickly Duke of Gloucester, at Mrs Davies' house nearby (a house on the site of the present Orleans House). Even earlier, back in the 1670s, and after the death of their mother Anne Hyde, Mary and Anne had spent 3 years with their governess, Lady Frances Villiers, and her husband Colonel Edward Villiers, at the old palace at Richmond.

It is common ground that the central block of the present day York House dates back to the 17th Century. But no one is exactly sure when the construction took place. One possible clue is to be found in Moses

---

*A more plausible story was advanced by J.H. Jesse in 1846 (*Memoirs of the Court . .* Vol. 1, p. 180). He claims that Princess Mary spent her first few years with her grandfather, Clarendon, at York House. This appears to have been amended in later editions, for the reference picked up by Barbara and Henri Van Zee (*William and Mary,* 1973, p. 57) has it that Mary occasionally visited her grandfather at York House from the old palace at Richmond until he went into exile in 1667. Unfortunately most authorities agree that Mary and Anne took up residence in Richmond after their mother's death in 1671. By then Clarendon was in exile in France.

Glover's map of 1635 (see Map 1) which shows a building under construction in the vicinity of what would be York House — the poles representing scaffolding — and marked "Mr Pecarnes". Certainly, the Pitcarnes held land in Twickenham by the 1630s. A Document of 1637 relating to that family refers to a "Capital messuage vocat Yorke farme".* As late as 1828, the earliest of the surviving title deeds now held by Richmond Council contains the crucial phrase "now or late called Yorkes farme or York House".

Unfortunately this does little more than tell us that we have the right site and that a house (part of the present building) may have come into existence by the 1630s. A better clue, perhaps, lies in the Survey of Lands in Twickenham in 1661. There against the name of the Earl of Manchester appear the words "his Great House he dwelling in". A Deed of 1656 and Isleworth Syon Manor Courtbooks link Pitcarne to Manchester, and a Deed of 1661 confirms that Manchester disposed of York Farm to the Hyde family. It is reasonable to assume that York House (that is to say, its central block) was in being by the late 1630s, and certainly not later than the 1660s.

To turn now, briefly, to the problem of the lands that went with the House. The original York family lands were scattered through Twickenham and neighbouring parishes. In the reign of Henry VIII the York Manor became a part of the Honour of Hampton as Crown property. Although portions of the Honour were often leased out to members of the Court or persons of eminence, the Honour came to be treated as part of the Queen's dower. Both Henrietta Maria and Catherine of Braganza held the Honour as part of their dower. As for Twickenham Manor itself, though regularly leased out from the mid-17th Century onwards, it remained Crown property until the middle of the 19th Century.

At the beginning of the 17th Century, in addition to scattered lands in Whitton and in neighbouring parishes, there were three sizeable blocks of Twickenham Manor lands: one linked to the Manor House (later called Arragon House), one linked to the Queen's farm (the lands around what is now called Orleans House),** and York Farm itself. At some point in the

*PRO, E 178/4499.
**For accounts of Arragon and Orleans Houses see BOTHLS Paper No. 60 and *The History of Orleans House* (1984).

2

17th Century, possibly as early at 1635, but certainly before 1665, York Farm was detached from the Twickenham (or York) Manor and became freehold but subject for a time to a yearly rent of £20. Inevitably the lands attached to York Farm or York House varied in extent as parcels were added or sold off over the years. For much of the time, the actual titles to the various parcels varied: in part freehold, in part copyhold of Twickenham Manor, and in part copyhold of Syon Manor. This remained the situation until the second half of the 19th Century. So land transactions involving York House could also involve the Court records of Isleworth and of Twickenham where copyhold lands were concerned. And, as will emerge later, this could involve conflicting Manorial customs: for whilst Twickenham Manor followed the practice of succession by primogeniture, Syon Manor followed the rule of "Borough English"; that is inheritance by the youngest son (unless the customary land had been later "surrendered" in court to the Tenant's Will).

A brief word also about the efficiency, or otherwise, of these two Manor Courts. Syon Manor, as befitted a large estate of long standing, kept increasingly detailed and up-to-date records of Court proceedings with usually two sessions annually, together with Special Courts as and when required. The Steward was always available for out of Court proceedings. The Fees, probably fixed in 1656 by the "Isleworth Peace", were modest and do not seem to have increased markedly over the years. As regards inheritance or transfer, the usual charge was a fine and a heriot (in money terms). Twickenham Manor, if the surviving records of the 18th and 19th Centuries are a fair guide, was in marked contrast. The Lord – or Lords – was a leasee for a term of years. The Stewards – often lawyers – were non-resident. The Jury (the Homage) was small in numbers, occasionally just a foreman (or forewoman) and one juryman. In contrast to Syon, the fees and fines were very high; as were the charges for wining and dining the Steward and the Jury. More importantly, the Court records are less detailed and long delays could occur before the Court registered a Tenant's death or a succession. Indeed, sometimes landholders even forgot to register changes in the Twickenham Manor Court.

Inevitably, these records vary in quality – and can appear contradictory and confusing. Nevertheless they are the best we have available as regards title to land. Together with the invaluable parish records, they are a prime source in seeking to fill in the numerous and puzzling gaps in the history of York House.

A NEW HOUSE FOR THE PITCARNES

If the view is correct that Glover's map of 1635 illustrated the building of a new house for "Mr Pecarnes", then it would seem that the central portion of York House (or rather York Farm as it was still called) was complete before the end of that decade. The Pitcarnes (the name is variously spelt Pitcarne, Pitcaine, Pitcairn, Pecarne, Pitkarne) had come to Twickenham in the early decades of the 17th Century. The first of that name was a Scotsman, Thomas Pitcarne, who acquired a reversion to York Farm in 1612. He hailed from Fife and had come south with the new King James I. Thomas may have moved to Twickenham subsequently to occupy property there: an inquisition of 1637 suggests that he had recently died. In the meantime Andrew Pitcarne, presumably a relative, had acquired the existing leases on York Farm and converted these into a freehold by 1640. He also held some copyhold land.* Andrew also had a lease of the Queen's Farm which may well have been the first residence of the Pitcarnes before the new house at York Farm had been completed. The Pitcarnes also held land in Whitton, perhaps representing detached lands belonging to one or both of these properties.

Andrew Pitcarne was also a Scot, the fifth son of the Laird of Forthar. As a boy he had been a page in the household of the infant Prince Charles and seems to have come to England with the Prince in about 1605. Thereafter Andrew Pitcarne remained a member of Charles' household. After Charles became Prince of Wales, Pitcarne became one of the Grooms of the Bedchamber, a post he continued to fill after Charles became King in 1625. This appointment brought with it a life pension of £500 a year and further marks of royal favour: Keeper of the King's Hawks, then Master Surveyor and Keeper of the King's Hawks, Hereditary Chief Falconer (a post he purchased off his eldest brother), a Gentleman Usher, a reversion to the Clerkship of the Crown in Chancery, and other positions of profit. In 1627 or 1628 Pitcarne secured "denization" by a royal warrant. Not

*The Syon Manor Courtbook for 24 May 1656 notes that Andrew Pitcarne was admitted to certain copyhold lands at a Court held on 18 October 1637.

content with these posts, Pitcarne followed the common practice of Court officials in indulging in business, often by means of monopolies (his colleague Endymion Porter, another of the six Grooms to the Bedchamber, got involved in such things as soap manufacturing to the detriment of the old established soap merchants of London and Bristol). Pitcarne's private dealings (backed by Crown licences) included fees on sea coal used in salt making, the collection (and retention) of outstanding fines due from Catholic recusants, checking (and being paid fees) on the abuses of goldsmiths, and supplying the Crown with gunpowder. In some of these activities Pitcarne went into partnership: his gunpowder enterprise saw him teamed up with Sir Arthur Mainwaring. The combination of pensions and fees from the various Crown posts he held, together with profits from his business enterprises, would have made Pitcarne a wealthy man and there were signs of this in the bequests made under his Will of 1640. But the Crown was not always prompt to pay its servants and sometimes Pitcarne was lending his master sums of money. By 1640 the Crown owed him at least £1000 and was also in arrears on his pension to the tune of £2000. Nevertheless, financially, Pitcarne was in a position to acquire land and to build a house. After all, his fellow Scot, the King's former whipping boy, William Murray, had moved into Ham House sometime between 1626 and 1637 (in the latter year he bought the house). Murray, who was later to become Earl of Dysart, was like Pitcarne another of the Grooms to the Bedchamber. Yet another senior Court official already lived in the vicinity. This was Sir John Suckling, who lived in Whitton. In addition to his Court duties (as a Secretary of State and then Controller of the Household) Sir John — whose son John was the poet — acted as a local J.P.

Pitcarne, too, was involved in local affairs. In May 1636 he was elected to the Twickenham Vestry: he took part in the election of two new members of Vestry in May 1640. In August that year he was a member of the commission appointed by the Vestry to make new assessments of the parish rates based on property or land. On 12 October 1640, Andrew Pitcarne made his Will. A few weeks later he was dead. His burial took place at Twickenham on 1 December 1640. By then, Pitcarne would have been in his early fifties.

His Will gives us some insight into his affairs. Charity, his wife, was the sister of Benjamin Tichbune (or Tichbourne) of Aldershot and was given the York Farm for the rest of her life. The reversion of this property was entailed to his son Charles and his male heirs. Andrew's daughters, Philipa and Charity were to have portions amounting to £1000 each (but half of these portions was in the form of debts owed by the Crown). In addition Philipa inherited a silver ladle valued at £50 whilst Charles was to have all the plate and linen at his mother's death, save for the gilt plate that was to be divided equally amongst the three children. Some of the Pitcarne relatives are also named, monetary legacies and gifts were made to them and to old friends of swords, belts, cloaks, hats, suits of clothes and other items. One suit of clothes was of grey trimmed with gold and "naigre"; another suit was trimmed with silver and gold.

Charity Pitcarne, Andrew's widow, having succeeded to York House (in "free . . . socage"), was shortly afterwards re-married, and became Dame Charity Poole. On her death in 1653, her children still being minors, Ludovic Carlile took over the task of carrying out the provisions of Andrew Pitcarne's Will. Perhaps the Pitcarnes were fortunate in that Andrew had died before the outbreak of the Civil War; or perhaps Charity's second husband had friends on the Parliamentary side, since they do not seem to have suffered from the effects of sequestration, such as befell so many royalists.

Charles Pitcarne, still a minor, inherited his father's entailed property. By 1656 he had come of age. An Indenture of 1 May 1656 between him and other parties, including Lancelot Lake and Richard Franklin (agents for the Earl of Manchester), was drawn up in order to stage a "Recovery", a fictitious legal action, to break the entail, and then sell "Yorke Farme" to the Earl. The Deed mentions that the lands attached to York House were bounded by certain "buttes" (old archery grounds) and by Fishers Lane (the lane later known as Dog Lane and now as Sion Road). The Recovery was to be taken in the Court of Chancery, but a similar action was also heard at the Syon Court Baron on 24 May 1656 immediately after Charles Pitcarne had been admitted to his late father's copyhold lands being of "full age". At the conclusion of the action, which in passing referred to the fact that the Earl of Manchester was already in occupation, the Earl's agents, Franklin and Lake, were admitted as the new customary tenants.

Charles Pitcarne, however, continued to live in Twickenham. In August

1657 the Vestry confirmed his right to a pew in the little Chancel "next above ye seate belonginge to ye Vicker". Charles then became a Church-warden together with Joseph Ashe in the years 1659 and 1660. In March 1661 his property in Twickenham was assessed at an annual rental value of £92 (including £10 for the house he was then living in at Whitton), the second highest valuation in the parish. His son, also called Charles, was buried in Twickenham in June 1661. By 1663, however, if not earlier, Charles Pitcarne had begun to sell off his land and the size of his property steadily diminished, a fact reflected in the Church rates he was assessed for: £1 in 1659, £2 (a triple rate) in 1660, 10s in 1661, 2s in 1671.* The last reference to him locally was the burial of James Pitcarne "son of Mr Charles" on 23 September 1675.

THE EARL OF MANCHESTER

Edward Montagu, the 2nd Earl of Manchester (1602-71) was in his fifties when he came to Twickenham. As a young man he had followed Prince Charles on that unsuccessful trip to Spain in search of a bride ("Castles in Spain" so the saying went — in Twickenham the church bells rang out in 1623 to welcome them home without a Spanish princess). Manchester, although a friend of Charles when the latter was a young prince, opposed him when King, and sided with Parliament during the Civil War. He was a commanding general first in East Anglia, then at Marston Moor and at the second battle of Newbury. He was, however, too moderate — "of a gentle and a generous nature, civilly bredd" according to Clarendon; "a soft and obliging temper and therefore universally beloved" in Bishop Burnet's view — for such troubled times and he opposed the trial of the King. On Charles' execution, Manchester went into virtual retirement. He had become Chancellor of Cambridge University in 1649 but was stripped of this office in 1651.

Of Manchester's stay in his great house in Twickenham there are a few scattered references. He had with him his third wife (in all he married five times). She was Essex Cheke, the widow of Sir Robert Bevil. The Twicken-ham parish registers record the birth of one daughter here, Lady Lucy in

*Charles Pitcarne's name also appears in the list of those assessed for the Poor Rate on 27 May 1672.

1655, and a son, George, in 1656. In all, Lady Manchester bore him eight
children, but these two, Lucy and George, seem to have been the youngest,
for she died here in the autumn of 1658. There is a hint of contagious
fever at work in York House. In the weeks preceding Lady Manchester's
death two of her servants were also buried in Twickenham; Henry
Ridgawaie on 12 September and Mrs Squier on 19 October, both servants
to the "Earll and Countis".

Nothing daunted, Manchester married shortly afterwards his fourth
wife, a widow, Elinor Wortley (Manchester was her fourth husband, so
they were well matched). She was still alive when Manchester gave up
York House in 1661.

The Church records have other references to Manchester's stay in
Twickenham. He paid £5 for a pew for his servants and £1-10s in rates in
1659. In July 1660 he paid a triple church rate of £3. More significant is
his appearance as the first named in the Parish Survey of 25 March 1661
(i.e. New Year's Day, Old Style). This survey was to value property and
houses for the purposes of assessing future Church and Poor Rates. The
basis of the assessment was to establish an annual rental value. Manchester
is shown as possessing only 13 acres of land with an annual value of £10,
whereas Sir Joseph Ashe held 193 acres valued at £42. But Manchester's
house — "his great house he dwelling in" — was assessed at £30, the
highest valuation in the Parish. Sir Joseph Ashe's house (in the vicinity of
Cambridge Park) only rated £20 and most other houses a lot less. Even
Captain Ells' "great new house" in the vicinity of what is now Orleans
House rated only a modest £7-10s valuation. York House was clearly a
very large house by the Twickenham standards of the 1660s.

The reason for Manchester's departure from Twickenham was that
with the Restoration of Charles II, he was again engaged at the centre of
public affairs. He had welcomed the King's return and was *persona grata*
at Court. Manchester immediately became involved in the trial of the
Regicides, and at the coronation of the King he bore the sword of State.
He was restored to his Chancellorship of the University of Cambridge,
and his Lord Lieutenancies in Northamptonshire and Huntingdonshire,
and he became Lord Chamberlain. During the Second Dutch War, in a time
of crisis, he raised a regiment of soldiers and resumed military duties. He
was also a Fellow of the Royal Society. In 1667 he took a fifth wife,
and died in 1671. He lies buried at Kimbolton in Huntingdonshire.

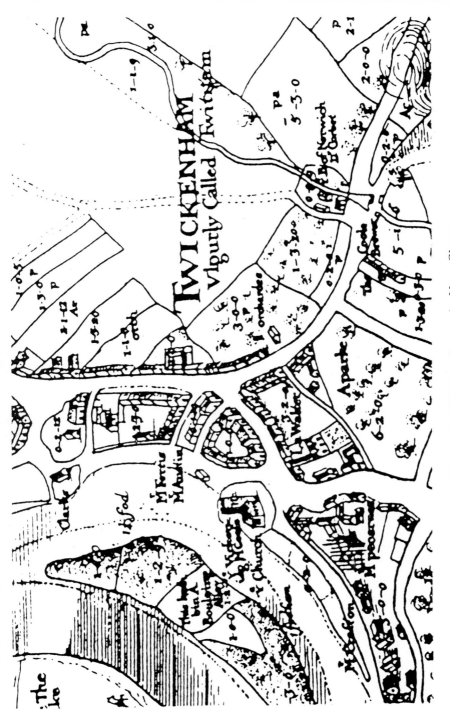

Map 1. *The area in 1635 from the map by Moses Glover*

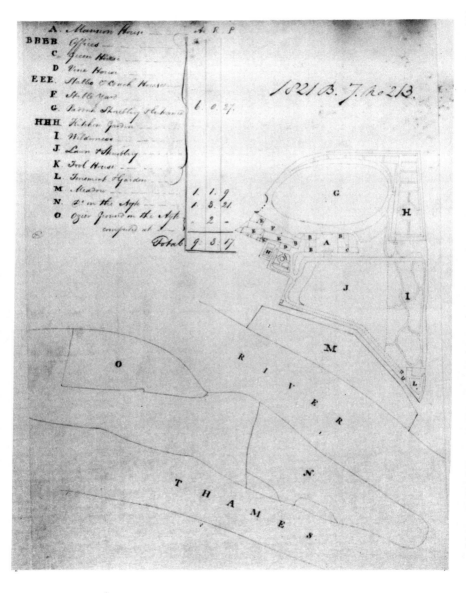

Map 2.   Sketch Map of the Estate in 1818
(By permission of the Greater London Record Office)

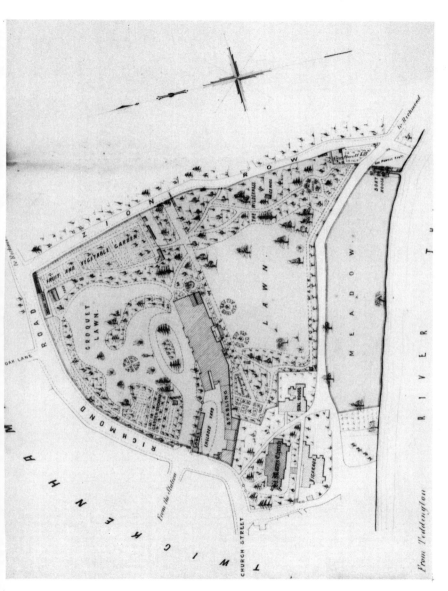

Map 3. Map of Estate 1876
(By permission of the Greater London Record Office)

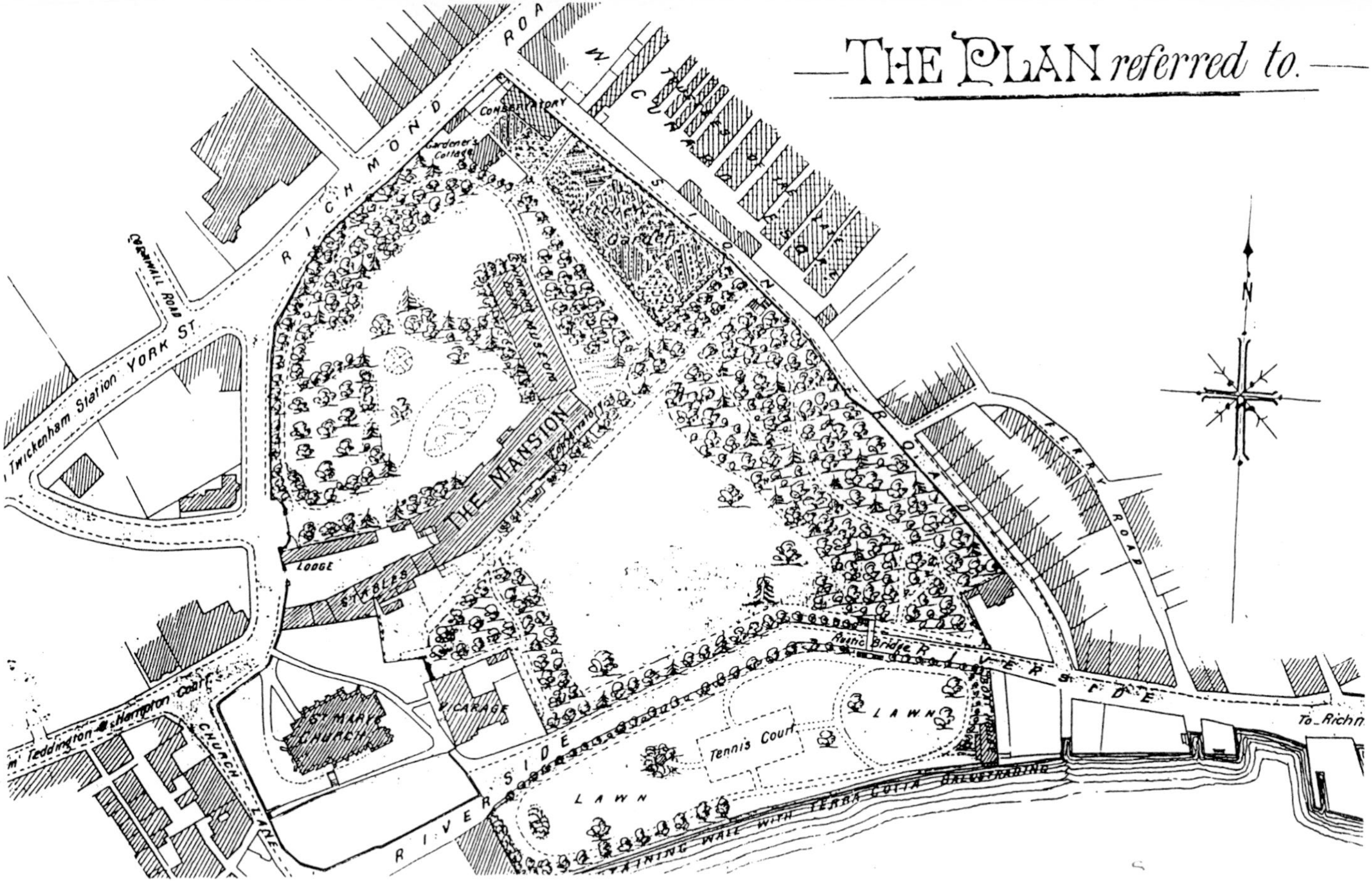

Map 4. House and Grounds in 1907

THE HYDES: THE EARL OF CLARENDON AND HIS SONS

The Restoration, which took the Earl of Manchester off to other pastures, brought Edward Hyde's family into contact with Twickenham. Hyde, whilst still in exile in Holland, had become Lord Chancellor to Charles II. Now in these "golden days", he returned with his King, ready to enjoy his own. Gifts and favours came in rapid succession. Hyde himself became Earl of Clarendon, and also Chancellor of Oxford University. His eldest son, Henry, took the courtesy title of Lord Cornbury. Then Manchester sold York House to the Hydes in 1661 — the price was £3,500 — the nominal owner was named in the title deeds as Lord Cornbury. The reasons for this are obscure, for it was Clarendon who paid for the house and also paid the Hearth Tax in 1664 and 1666.* This may have been a temporary measure, since a later deed — relating to the Manor of Twickenham rather than to the house — shows that the Manor was assigned to Edward Earl of Clarendon in 1665. This assignment was for a term of ten years after the expiry of the current term of 21 years "now expired" and adds "besides £20 fee farme rent for Yorke farme heretofore part of the said Manor". This does suggest that by 1665 both Manor and York House were regarded as Clarendon's to dispose of rather than belonging to Lord Cornbury. When Clarendon made his Will in 1666 (20 January 1665 O.S.**), he gave to his second son Laurence (later to become Earl of Rochester):

> "my landes and house at Twitnam . . . whether copyhold or otherwise which God knowes as much at least as my present state will bear without too much hurting my other children but if it please God to bless me with many more years of life I hope to inlarge his fortune"***

---

*37 hearths in 1664 and 43 in 1666.

**O.S. = Old Style (the year beginning on 25 March and 11 days behind the present Calendar.

***Ollard, *Clarendon and his Friends,* p. 348. It is just possible that the wording of the original (MS CLAR 84) could read "my landes and houses" but this does not seem to be the generally accepted view. Clarendon's subsequent Will written in exile in 1674 relates solely to his books and papers, makes his sons Henry and Laurence executors, and leaves to them the care of his other children. In so far as York House and Twickenham were concerned, Henry and Laurence adhered to the spirit of the 1666 Will.

Despite later changes in that fortune, this intention of Clarendon's seems to have been fulfilled both in terms of York House and of the lease on the Manor of Twickenham (the house had, of course, become detached from the Manor sometime earlier and stood on freehold land).

There remains the puzzle as to whether Clarendon or his sons ever actually used the house. Such evidence as there is, is circumstantial, not direct. It is possible that the original arrangement was to make provision for Lord Cornbury who was newly married and had a young family. Cornbury himself later confirmed that his father paid for the house. When in London, Clarendon used Worcester House and during the years 1664-66 was having built, off Piccadilly, the princely and expensive Clarendon House. No sooner was it complete than Clarendon had been driven into exile once more.

But to return to the question of York House. Clarendon wrote a letter from Twickenham (the house is unspecified) to Sir George Downing in July 1662. He was certainly in Twickenham in January 1666: again in August 1666 a Franciscan friar, writing from Dublin, regrets the writer's failure to call on Clarendon when the latter had been in Twickenham some 13 months earlier. In April 1666 the Twickenham Vestry minutes record that the Vicar, Dr Hobson, had sought the Chancellor's assent for Edward Gray to be Vicar's Warden. Gray seems to have been a member of Clarendon's household, possibly his local Steward. Permission was not given since Dr Hobson's second choice, George Bartlet, was subsequently made Vicar's Warden for that year, together with Thomas Parker, the People's Warden. Clarendon clearly took a close interest in local affairs.

At this time Clarendon was absorbed in weighty affairs of state with the Second Dutch War raging and London ravaged by the plague (in Twickenham there were 24 plague deaths). Another disaster struck the capital on 2 September 1666 when the Great Fire broke out. Clarendon, who had still been based at Worcester House when the Fire broke out, wrote to his friend the Duke of Ormonde on 22 September about the event. His wife had been in a "terrible apprehansyn" and "caused all my goodes to be throwne into lighters for Twitnam and into cartes for my new house and other places".*

*Ollard, *op. cit.,* pp. 274-275.

10

In the Spring of 1667 another local difficulty arose in Twickenham in which Clarendon's servant Edward Gray was again involved. The Vestry minutes of 9 May 1667 note that Edward Gray having complained that "ye Erle of Clarendons pew" for his servants in the gallery had been taken away from him by the Churchwardens,

"it was decided that noe person should sitt in ye pew but by leave of my Lord Clarendon or his servants".

This was the same pew that the Earl of Manchester had previously paid £5 for some years earlier.

One other piece of evidence is available in the Vestry records. From April 1661 until 1667, Clarendon is shown as paying the Twickenham Church and Poor rates, being listed either as the Earl of Clarendon or, more usually, as "Lord Chancellor".

Clarendon's days of power, however, were numbered. He fell from favour and was dismissed from the Lord Chancellorship in August 1667 and even threatened with impeachment once Parliament re-assembled. His daughter Anne, wife of the Duke of York and mother of two future Queens, could do nothing to save him. The King was willing to sacrifice him rather than court unpopularity; so Clarendon sought refuge in flight. Pepys on 6 December 1667 first heard details of the flight from a colleague, Sir John Minnes, "who tells me that my Lord Clarendon did go away in a custom-house boat and is now at Callis". Later that day, in conversation with Sir William Coventry, Pepys learnt that,

"On Sunday his [Clarendon's] coach and people about it went to Twittenham and the world thought he had been there".

These, then, are the bare bones of evidence linking Clarendon to his House in Twickenham. For the rest — its convenience to Hampton Court when the King was there — it is a matter of speculation.

Clarendon was to remain in exile on the continent until his death at Rouen on 9 December 1674.* His Twickenham house remained, pre-

---

*A summary of "evidences" prepared by John Clutterbook in 1671 relates to the title deeds of the various Hyde properties held at Clarendon House. These include a list of Deeds relating to York Farm and other Twickenham lands. Clutterbook was Cornbury's man of business. He is referred to in a letter Clarendon *[continued over*

sumably under the control of his eldest son Henry, who with his brother Laurence became executor to his father's Will. An entry in the Syon Manor Courtbook for 18 October 1676 refers to an earlier transaction of 3 July 1675 and then registers the surrender of certain copyhold lands, formerly held by Clarendon (i.e. Henry) to "Hon Lawrence Hide". This would be in keeping with Edward Hyde's Will of 1666, and seems to be borne out by the transfer of the lease of Twickenham Manor by Henry to his brother Laurence at about the same time. A later Deed of 1689 contains the revealing phrase to the effect that the right title interest and term of years in Twickenham Manor had been vested in the Earl of Rochester (as Laurence Hyde had now become),

> "by assignment of Henry Earle of Clarendon Executor of the last Will and Testament of Edward Earle of Clarendon his father . . ."

York House must have passed to Rochester about the same time. This seems to be confirmed by the entries in the Churchwardens' accounts relating to the Poor and Church rates for these years. In 1668, Lord Cornbury's name replaces that of the 1st Earl of Clarendon, followed in subsequent years by three names that can fairly be assumed to be short term tenants: the Countess of Anglesey in 1669, Lord Arundell (of Trerice) in 1670-73 (in his last year marked "gone away"), followed by Lady Falmouth in 1674. In 1675, however, the name Clarendon reappears (this, of course, would be Henry), followed by Laurence Hyde in 1676. Thereafter Laurence Hyde regularly appears until 1682 when he is listed as Earl of Rochester.

Laurence Hyde rose rapidly in the world to become Viscount Hyde in 1681 and then Earl of Rochester in the following year. He proved useful to Charles II both as a diplomat and then as a Minister and earned the barbed praise of Dryden as "Hushai" in the satirical poem "Absalom and Achitophel", which he published in November 1681.* Rochester

---

continued] wrote to Henry in April 1674 which mentions that Laurence is to have the rents from "Twitnam". It appears that York House was finally detached from Twickenham Manor in 1661. This applied only to the freehold.

*   "Hushai the friend of David in distress,
    In public storms of manly steadfastness;
    . . . . .
    His frugal care supplied the wanting throne,
    Frugal for that, but bounteous of his own."

remained immersed in politics up to his death in 1711, enjoying both influence and power as an uncle to Queen Mary II and later Queen Anne. He certainly appears to have used his Twickenham house on occasions. His young son Edward was buried in Twickenham on 7 January 1680 O.S. But Rochester eventually began to consider disposing of the house. In May 1686 his brother, Henry, now Lord Lieutenant of Ireland, wrote from Dublin to Laurence about various family matters, adding,

> "I heartily wish you a good chapman [trader, dealer] for Twickenham but you will not, I doubt, get what it cost my father, who paid roundly for all his purchases besides what he laid out upon them afterwards, which will not make them yield anything the more."

In 1689 Rochester found a buyer and sold York House and also separately his lease of years for the Manor of Twickenham. His nephew, Lord Cornbury, had some years earlier acquired a house in Petersham. This house Rochester now took over and, in 1692, set about rebuilding it. The Hyde connection with Twickenham was at an end. But Henry's prophecy of 1686 proved correct: York House had cost his father £3,500; 28 years later Rochester only got £3,000 for it.

THE TUFTONS

The new owner of York House was Sir Charles Tufton. The Deed of Sale is dated 10 April in the first year of William and Mary's reign (that is 1689; some clerk confusedly wrote 1688 on the back of the Deed). This was subsequently reinforced by Tufton's admission as customary tenant for the copyhold at the Syon Manor Court of 24 January 1689 O.S. (i.e., 1690). The court entry specified 4 copyhold parcels of land. A similar procedure must have been followed for Twickenham copyhold lands, but Courtbooks for these years have not survived.

Little is known about Sir Charles. The Deed of Sale refers to him as of Lincoln's Inn Fields* which may indicate that he followed the legal profession. He was a grandson of the 1st Earl of Thanet and was knighted in 1666 (he was the only Sir Charles Tufton to be listed in Shaw's *Knights*

---

*His father, Cecil, died at Lincoln's Inn Fields in June 1682 and was buried in the family vault at Rainham, Kent. The House was probably No. 43, Lincoln's Inn Fields. (*Survey of London,* Vol. III, p. 53. Robert Pocock, *Memorials of the Tufton Family* (1800)).

of England, and if Shaw is correct, then Tufton came from Costan in Gloucestershire). By the time he came to Twickenham he was married, his wife being variously named as Alice, Alief, Eleph, and Ayliffe (this last is the most usual form). In his Will, Sir Charles refers to her as "my dear and loving wife".

During the 1690s seven children were born to the Tuftons and christened in St Mary's Church, Twickenham. These were Aliefe, Diana, Shalot, Mary, Katherin, Christian,* and Thomas. Catherine died at the age of two, and Mary at the age of 14, both being buried at Twickenham. There was also an older son, Cecil, who later appears as Lady Tufton's executor in the Syon Courtbooks of 1726. Finally there is an "Hon Mrs Tufton" who sometime in the 18th Century gave £21 to the Church, but whether she was connected to Sir Charles and his family is not known.

Sir Charles Tufton died in May 1708** and Lady Tufton was admitted in his place as copyhold tenant of Syon Manor at a Court held on 13 October 1708. By this stage, the Tuftons held 9 parcels of copyhold land in addition to the freehold of York House and the copyhold of Twickenham Manor. Amongst these lands were five messuages which later came to be called "Tufton's Court" and subsequently became a permanent part of the York House estate.

What little we know about the Tuftons at York House is largely thanks to that indefatigable letter writer, Lady Wentworth, mother of Lord Raby (later Earl of Strafford) who, in Queen Anne's reign, lived during the summers at her son's house on the Twickenham riverside. I can do no better than quote from Donald Simpson's fascinating account of Lady Wentworth in Twickenham.*** On 14 July 1710, Lady Tufton had just buried her daughter, Mary. Lady Wentworth, writing to her son, reported this sad event and added more practically that Lady Tufton still had five handsome daughters left:

*Christian was, in fact, Christiana. She died in September 1783 (*Gentleman's Magazine,* 1783). Her sister Charlotte died in 1767.
**Buried at Maidstone (John Le Neve, *Monumenta Anglicana,* Vol. 4, p. 163). But Lady Tufton's Will says Rainham.
***BOTLHS Paper No. 35, *Twickenham Society in Queen Anne's Reign.*

"For five thousand pd you may by her hous, and one or twoe may be bated if
you will take a daughter; it is the most convenyents hous I ever see, all the
offisis wonderfull good, it was the Queen's grandfather's, it stands in the midle
of a garden, its a charming review, thear is thre ways for a coach to com to it."

A few days later Lady Wentworth wrote of the sorrowing Tufton family's
entrance into St Mary's Church:

"thear could not be a more dismall mallancoly sight then poor Lady Tufton
led by her eldist son, the eldist daughter following led by the other, and the
other fower daughters following one after the other, al in long scarfs and alla-
mode huods over their faicis, not a bit to be seen of them. Soe they sat al
churchtime, and a very hot day. I wonder they was not smothered."

Some years earlier, before her husband's death, poor Lady Tufton's family
provided Lady Wentworth with yet another item of gossip. A neighbour,
the widowed Lady Derwentwater, was about to marry her third husband
in August 1707 but found the Tufton children present in church; where-
upon Lady Derwentwater,

"turned Lady Tuften's children out of the church, and said she would not be
marryed tel they went out. She was marryed in whit sattin."

Some of the Tufton connections with the Church caused less gossip. When
the old Church fell down in April 1713 both Lady Tufton and her son
Cecil pledged £50 towards the rebuilding.

One other link with the Tuftons locally may have derived from old
ties of friendship between families. Captain John Gray* had been admitted
as a customary tenant of Syon Manor in October 1718. During the next
few years five of his children were baptised in St Mary's Church. On 3
March 1724 O.S., a son of Captain John and his wife Elizabeth was
christened Tufton Gray. Presumably one of the Tuftons acted as god-
parent. Captain Gray, of course, was responsible for the building of
Montpelier and Sion Rows.

It is not certain when Lady Tufton died, but it probably was early in
the year 1720. Her copyhold lands in Syon Manor were not transferred

---

*In addition to Edward Gray, the servant of the 1st Earl of Clarendon, there was
one Richard Gray, who, together with Richard Genew, had acted for the Earl of
Rochester in formally handing over York Farm to Sir Charles Tufton in May
1689.

until 1726, when her executors, her son Cecil* and Robert Meese submitted her Will (dated 27 April 1719) to the Manor Court. Lady Tufton in her Will instructed her executors to sell her lands both in Middlesex and in Essex as soon as was conveniently possible. A similar entry at a slightly earlier date appears in the earliest of the Twickenham Manor Courtbooks to have survived.

Over the next few years her wishes were carried out and the Tufton lands were sold off. At some stage the York House estate was also disposed of.

Lady Tufton's Will is worth further mention for the light it throws upon her character. Her husband, Sir Charles, had left everything to her absolutely since he trusted her implicitly. She made various bequests: her son Thomas was to have £1400 and, in lieu of his Godfather's gift of £100, all his mother's personal goods and chattels. She added rather sharply that she had spent many times that sum on him already. Her eldest daughter Elizabeth received a portion of £600; the four other girls got portions of £400 each. There were other gifts: "Dear Aunt Sarah Duncombe" was to get 20 guineas and separate arrangements were made for the distribution of mourning rings. Robert Meese was given £100 for his trouble and the residue went to Charles. But clearly the Will only dealt with part of the Tufton property for Lady Tufton notes that the main provisions for her and her late husband's estate had already been dealt with in a family Indenture of 13 and 14 August 1717: the details of these arrangements are not known but almost certainly included York House.

Finally Lady Tufton left instructions for her funeral. It was to be a quiet one at Rainham where her husband was buried. There was to be but one hearse and one coach and no rooms were to be hung in mourning. Her final message to her children was simple:

"I doe hereby enjoin them all to serve God and live in peace and amity with one another which alone can make them happy."

Certainly Lady Tufton was a woman of considerable personality. As late as the 1740s, York House was known locally as "Lady Tufton's".

---

*Cecil Tufton appears to have entered University College, Oxford, in Apil 1707 aged 18. He died in his forty-first year on 11 August 1728 and is believed to have been buried in the family vault at Rainham in Kent.

THE 18th CENTURY AND A PERIOD OF CONFUSION

Lady Tufton died in about 1720. Thereafter confusion reigned, or so it
seems to anyone trying to make sense of the contemporary title deeds.
What appears to have happened is that in June 1720 Cecil Tufton and
Robert Meese (executors to Lady Tufton's Will of 27 April 1719) together
with Thomas Tufton, Lady Tufton's youngest child, sold "Yorkes ffarme"
together with its lands to Thomas Vernon of Twickenham Park. Vernon
then appears to have entered into a mortgage arrangement with Cecil
Tufton and Meese to the tune of £1575, one of a number of mortgages
that Vernon took out in the process of some large scale land transactions.
In 1723 Vernon made his Will: he died in August 1726. He left his widow
Jane and his three daughters — Jane, Annabella and Matilda — mortgages
totalling over £9000 and unpaid legacies left to his daughters from a
deceased family friend worth a further £1500 (unpaid, that is, by Vernon;
he seems to have used the money for his own transactions). In addition
he had committed his estate to find portions for each of his daughters at
the age of 21 (or when married) worth £5000; that is £15,000 for the
three. Jane Vernon, his widow and executor, in managing the family
affairs found it necessary to borrow more money from a relative, Anna
Catherina Vernon, a spinster. In 1727, an indenture of sale and lease and
release indicates that "Yorke ffarme" and at least some of the land
attached to it had been transferred to Jane Vernon. There is a suggestion
— no more — that she may have moved into York House (the indenture
states that the house and lands were "*now* in possession of said Jane
Vernon or her undertenants"). The document also implies that the some
time between roughly 1720 and 1727 the property had been,

> "late . . . in the tenure or occupation of the Honorable Richard Edgcumbe Esq*
> afterwards of the Right Honorable Elizabeth Countess Dowager of Exeter and
> since of his Grace the present Duke of Rutland."

It has to be said at once that none of these names have appeared in such
earlier deeds as have been traced, although the names are repeated parrot-
wise in later deeds. There is, of course, no certainty that any of these
people dwelt in York House. But the probability is that they may have

*The Church Rates for 1718 list an "Edgcomb Esq".

been very short term tenants.

But who were they? Richard Edgcumbe (1680-1758) was a West-countryman with considerable political influence who managed the Cornish boroughs during Sir Robert Walpole's time. He became the 1st Lord Mount Edgcumbe in 1742. He may have been distantly related to the Vernons of Twickenham Park since his first wife, Matilda Furnese, was the granddaughter of one Sir Thomas Vernon.* Matilda died aged 22 in 1721. Lady Exeter was probably the second wife of John Cecil, 6th Earl of Exeter. He died in December 1721. His widow, the daughter of Sir John Barlow Bt. had married Lord Exeter in 1699, bringing with her a fortune of £1200 a year and a capital sum of £10,000. She died in London in November 1723. As for the "present" Duke of Rutland, this would have been John Manners (1696-1779), the 3rd Duke, who had succeeded to the title in February 1721.

As has already been mentioned, it was not until 5 October 1726 that Cecil Tufton got around to informing the Syon Manor Court of the death of his mother and securing admission to the copyhold portion of the York House lands, which he immediately surrendered to the Vernons. These parcels went first to the Vernon daughters but they, in turn, transferred them back to their mother, Jane Vernon.

If, then, Vernon's widow, Jane, chose to move from her home at Twickenham Park to York House, it cannot have been for long. At some point in the 1730s a dispute arose between her and her relative Anna Catherina, who had been living with the family, and they split up. The debts then owing to Anna Catherina now entered into the dispute. Clearly Jane Vernon was pressed for ready money, for the death of her eldest daughter Jane in 1732 had further complicated matters. The daughter Jane had left her portion (as yet probably unpaid) to be shared between her sisters Matilda and Annabella (Annabella's share being placed in her mother's charge as a trust). At some date before 1738, Mrs Vernon sold York House to Elizabeth, the wife of Pawlett St John of Dogmersfield in Hampshire. Subsequently, in 1743, the Vernons sold off Twickenham Park for £13,000 to the Earl of Mountrath. A portion of the York House

---

*A party to one of the Deeds relating to the property of the Vernons of Twickenham Park was Sir Charles Vernon of Farnham, in Surrey.

lands, however, the five messuages known as Tufton Court, was retained
for the time being, together with a large number of other parcels of
Vernon land in Twickenham that had been acquired over the past years.

Mrs Vernon died on 18 January 1741 O.S. and such property as was
left went to Annabella and Matilda in equal and joint shares. They were
admitted as customary tenants of the Syon Manor on 21 April 1742.
Twickenham Manor had not got round to recording the death of Thomas
Vernon until 1741, but reacted to the death of Jane Vernon more swiftly.
The two sisters were duly admitted as tenants to the Twickenham Manor
in April 1743. Subsequently these two heiresses — their holdings of land
in this parish were very considerable — married: Matilda to Charles
Repington and Annabella to William A'Court. Both husbands were also
admitted as tenants by courtesy to their wives' copyhold lands. In 1750
and 1751 the sisters' joint and equal shares in Tufton Court were transferred to Harry Waller of Lincoln's Inn, who was also a resident of
Twickenham. He, however, may have acted simply as an agent, for in
July 1751 he transferred Tufton Court back to the new owner — and
occupant — of York House.

It is now necessary to retrace our steps to establish how the latest
owner of York House had got there. By 1738 York House and a portion
of its lands had been sold by Mrs Vernon to Mrs Elizabeth St John. That
lady, however, died shortly afterwards, and her husband inherited the
house. Pawlett St John sold York House (still referred to as "York
ffarme") in April 1738 to Joshua Naylor, a jeweller of Covent Garden.
Naylor, in turn, towards the end of our period of confusion, sold York
House in July 1746, but more of that shortly. Suffice it to say that in
all these complex property transactions it is impossible to say who was
actually living in York House at any given time. Indeed, it is quite possible
that for long periods of time the house remained empty. The probabilities
are that at various times between 1720, or a little earlier, and 1742 or so,
the house was occupied for varying periods by Richard Edgcumbe, Elizabeth Dowager Countess of Exeter, John Duke of Rutland, Mrs Jane
Vernon, and Elizabeth St John and her husband Pawlett St John. The
Vestry records show that Pawlett St John paid Church rates from 1734
to 1736. Joshua Naylor (or Nailor), the jeweller, was almost certainly
an absentee.

19

One final twist to all this confusion. In 1742 York House was put up for sale, presumably by Joshua Naylor. Nothing came of this, but the advertisement at least gives us some account of the House as it then was. The auctioneer was Mr Cock of Covent Garden, Naylor's home district. The curious thing was that the house was now called "York House" but was also referred to as still being "commonly call'd Lady Tufton's". Its lands were principally freehold save for "the Meadow and part of the Stable-Yard" which were copyhold of Twickenham Manor. (There is no reference to Syon copyhold land for the simple reason that such land had been detached from the York House grounds back in the 1730s and was not reunited to the estate until the 1750s.) For the rest, the advertisement described the property in the following terms:

"situate on a rising gravelly soil, fronting the River Thames with a Piece of Meadow Ground before it, having a most beautiful and extensive Prospect every way.

The House is built of Brick, in a very strong, regular, and elegant Taste, consisting of a noble Hall and Drawing Room of 30 Feet by 20 with four other large Parlours, Waiting Rooms etc. And on the first Floor a State-Room and Drawing-Room of equal Dimensions with the Hall, and four Bed-Chambers about twenty feet square, with Dressing Rooms etc both Apartments about 12 Feet high, with a magnificent Stair-Case, several of the Rooms are stucco'd and ornamented with carv'd and gilt Cornices, with very good Floors; the whole being in excellent Repair.

The second Floor consists of five good Bed-Chambers, a Wardrobe, a large Gallery of 70 Feet, stucco'd and back Stairs to several Apartments.

There are Out-Offices of all sorts, as a very large Kitchen, Servants Hall, Housekeeper's and Butler's Room, Larder, Pantries, Brewhouse, Bakehouse, and exceeding good Cellaring; with noble and convenient Court-Yards, two Coach-houses and Stabling for 13 Horses, a large Barn, etc.

The Gardens are beautifully dispos'd both for Pleasure and Use, and eminent for their great Variety of choice Fruit, with a most delightful Grove, a Terras and Wilderness Walks, enrich'd with two fine Greenhouses etc."

Fig. 5.   Aerial view of the York House area c.1920

Fig. 6. Engraving of York House by J.P. Malcolm c.1808

Fig. 7. Engraving of York House from the Auction Catalogue of 1873

*Fig. 8. Edward Montagu, Earl of Manchester
engraving by T.A. Dean after Sir Peter Lely*

*Fig. 9. Edward Hyde, Earl of Clarendon
engraving by J. Thomson after Sir Peter Lely*

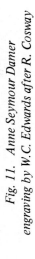

Fig. 11. Anne Seymour Damer
engraving by W.C. Edwards after R. Cosway

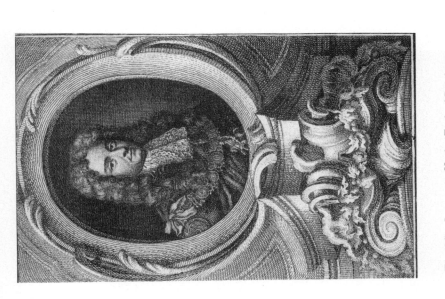

Fig. 10. Laurence Hyde, Earl of Rochester

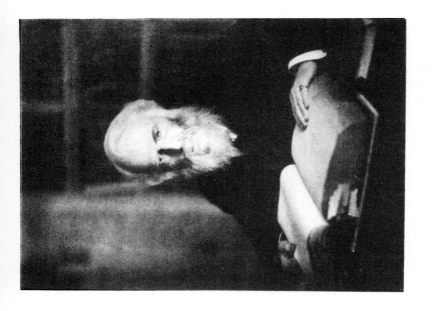

Fig. 13.   Mountstuart Grant Duff

Fig. 12.   Comte de Paris
photograph by Walery, 1889

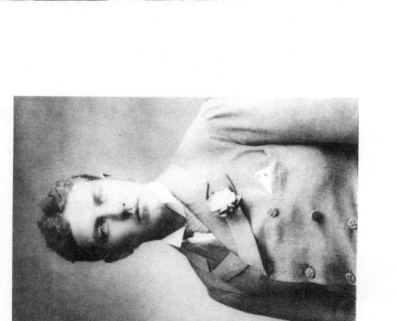

Fig. 15. Sir Ratan and Lady Tata

Fig. 14. Duc d'Orleans
Photograph by Walery, 1889

Fig. 16. The riverside meadow c. 1890

Fig. 17. Front view of York House 1906, showing the portico (now removed)

Fig. 18. Fleur de Lys ornamentations

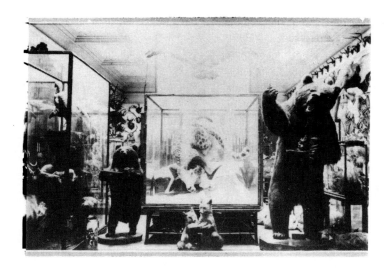

Fig. 19. The Museum established by the Duc d'Orleans

Fig. 20. The Swimming Pool (converted to Hall after 1924)

Fig. 21.   The Loggia

Fig. 22.   The Salon c.1906

Fig. 23. Group taken at the opening of York House, 16 November 1926

*Front row (left to right): E.G. Stray, Town Clerk; Alderman E.C. Dyer; Queen Augusta;
The Duke of York; Dr J.R. Leeson, Charter Mayor; the Duchess of York; King Manuel;
Sir William Joynson-Hicks, M.P.; the Rev. W.P. Cole Sheane, Vicar of Twickenham*

JAMES WHITCHURCH AND JAMES WEBBER

It is with some relief that we can turn from a period of confusion to one of certainty. An Indenture of 15 July 1746 records the transfer of "Yorks ffarm" from Joshua Naylor the jeweller of Covent Garden to James Whitchurch, then of Copthall Street near the Royal Exchange. Two years later, the first of the surviving Poor Rates books held by Twickenham Library lists James Whitchurch as paying rates in the Parish (with a Mrs Ann Whitchurch also paying rates for a separate but unidentified dwelling; possibly she was James Whitchurch's mother*). At the Twickenham Manor Court on 31 May 1748, James Whitchurch was also admitted to certain copyhold lands that had belonged to Pawlett St John. Then, in July 1751, Whitchurch acquired that detached portion of the York House ground by the transfer of the five freehold messuages called "Tufton Court" from Harry Waller. Finally, the last element in this legal jigsaw was put in place when the Syon copyhold lands were transferred from Harry Waller — he had received them from the Vernon sisters — to Whitchurch at a Manor Court held on 1 April 1752. As a result the York House grounds more or less as we know them today — just under 10 acres in all — had been finally brought together. Subsequently Whitchurch did make a minor alteration when, in 1754, he surrendered one copyhold messuage abutting on St Mary's Churchyard to William Ryder and Harry Waller in trust for the Parish. This was done at the Manor Court on 21 January 1754. At the same time the Lord and Lady of Syon Manor granted a piece of waste ground to the Parish (a tablet in the churchyard wall commemorates the gift). Both land transfers were for the purpose of enlarging the churchyard, which was still the Parish's burial ground. It is perhaps worth adding that Waller and Whitchurch were in turn Churchwardens at St Mary's: Whitchurch as Vicar's Warden in 1750 and People's Warden in 1751, and Waller as Vicar's Warden in 1752 and People's Warden in 1753. As for William Ryder, he too was a Churchwarden having partnered both men in the years 1751 and 1752.

We get a glimpse of James Whitchurch from his Will written in December 1782, to which four codicils were added between January 1784 and

*If so, did she live in Langham Cottage? And is this the origin of the local oral tradition that the cottage was once the Dower House?

June 1785. In 1782 he had at least 9 servants, including a coachman, that he thought worth naming in his Will; by 1785 that number had been reduced to seven. Whitchurch was a good if strict master: he left legacies of between £100 and £200 to the servants he had named (but swiftly removed their names if they chose to leave him). He also made provision for at least 8 godchildren, numerous relatives (not least his "dear nephew" Henry Hoare) and a number of friends — three of these being clergymen — or their children. Most of his money appears to have been held as cash in the bank or in bonds and annuities, but in addition to his real estate, i.e. York House, he held shares in the Bristol Brass Battery and Wire Company. His old London address — Copthall Street near the Royal Exchange — suggests that he had formerly been engaged in business in the City. Some idea of his wealth can be gauged from the fact that his monetary bequests alone totalled over £18,000. Henry Hoare, his nephew, who was to be his executor together with the Reverend Dr Morrice D.D., was also to inherit the bulk of his estate.

Whitchurch was concerned with charitable work; he names seven charities in his Will including £50 for Twickenham Charity School and £50 for the poor householders of this parish. But his largest charitable bequest was for the blind. Originally in 1782 he set aside £4,000 for this, but later increased the gift to £10,000 in January 1784. He was clearly an "earnest" man in the 18th Century sense of the word: not only did he have a number of clerical friends — and also one who was a Quaker — but he earmarked £400 for the purchase of religious books. Ill fortune, however, dogged his last days. His "dear nephew" died early in 1785, and by June of that year Whitchurch had suffered a severe financial loss so that the residue of his estate was "considerably diminished".

There is little else known about Whitchurch. It is curious to note that none of the artists who had painted in the vicinity of Twickenham during the first 80 years of the 18th Century ever recorded a view of York House. This was the case with Tillemans, whose view from Richmond Hill in the 1730s shows us so much local detail yet hides York House in a copse of trees (was this the "Wilderness" so frequently mentioned in later title deeds?). Nor did Heckel think York House worth while; the same is true of Samuel Scott who lived close by in the Manor House opposite the Church. Yet Scott records the more humble buildings on Twickenham's riverside. Was it that York House had ceased to be fashionable or that its owners did not command sufficient rank? Or was it more simply that the House was too often left empty? It is not until the end of Whitchurch's life that we have any picture of York House (Figure 1). York House appears in a view of the whole Twickenham Riverside in a watercolour by an amateur artist, Edward Ironside, painted in 1786.

Ironside was also the earliest of the Twickenham historians, who published in 1797 a *History and Antiquities of Twickenham.* Hopelessly inaccurate in parts — he started the legends about Queen Anne and York House — he is of much greater value in dealing with matters of which he was an eye-witness. The son of a former Lord Mayor of London, and himself a one time employee of the Honorable East India Company, Ironside lived in Twickenham for many years, latterly in a house in Sion Row. He died in Twickenham in 1803 aged 67. What is of particular interest to us is his account of York House which appears in the book he published in 1797. It was originally written whilst Whitchurch was still alive, although Ironside updated it slightly for the purposes of publication.

Ironside starts by referring to the house as "previously called 'York-Place' ". He then gives a colourful, but inaccurate, account of the house's earlier history:

> "I am inclined to think this house, from its name, was once the residence of James Duke of York . . . as his two daughters, Mary and Anne . . . were nursed in it, and that his highness on his marriage resigned it in favour of his father-in-law."

Ironside then turns to topics of which he had first hand knowledge:

> "The situation of this house is exceedingly pleasant; it has two fronts, the principal one faces the Thames, but is placed at such a distance as not to be subject to any inconveniences from its overflowing. The lawn before it is extensive; at the bottom of which is a terrace walk of gravel the whole length of the garden. On one side of the lawn is a grove of elms, with serpentine walks, and a small summer house, from which is a very pleasing view up the river. The other looks upon some inclosed grounds for pasturage. The house is of brick, well built and convenient. The rooms are most of them small, except the two halls which are about 36 feet long, 20 broad, and about 16 high, and are separated by an arch; that to the river serving as a drawing room, the other as a passage room for company. Over these is the winter drawing room and bed-chambers. The floor is oak inlaid.

23

> There are a few good pictures; views of Italy by Canaletti, some pleasing
> landscapes by Zucharelli, and a beautiful portrait in crayons of Lady Frances
> Shirley, when young.
>
> This house is now the property of James Whitchurch Esq."

There was, of course, one other possible eyewitness — Horace Walpole.
But in all the voluminous correspondence he has left there is nothing
save a passing reference. Writing to Lady Ossory in 1779, Walpole
comments on the "very significant tempest" with which that year
started so that the roads were strewn with tiles and bricks and trees and
even "entire garden walls" as was the case with Mr Whitchurch in
Twickenham.

Whitchurch died some time between June 1785 and February 1786. On
19 April 1786 the Syon Manor Court admitted the executors of his Will to
the copyhold lands he had held. A similar admission was made in the
Twickenham Manor Court on 17 May 1786. One feature of the Syon
Court proceedings is of interest as being a new departure. This was an
entry in the Court records of an "Acknowledgement of Free Tenure" for:

> "certain Freehold Lands and tenements in the said manor which were formerly
> Lady Tufton's by Fealty Suit of Court and the yearly rent of One shilling and
> three pence half penny, and they paid the Lord for the Relief [1s 3½d] . . . but
> their fealty was respited."

The three executors for Whitchurch's estate were now the Reverend
William Morrice, James Taggart, and William Addison. Taggart was one
of Whitchurch's many godchildren and was the new beneficiary for the
residue of the estate under the terms of the Will; Addison was the only
executor living in Twickenham. He had spent the last few years living with
Whitchurch at York House.

It would appear that York House remained unoccupied for the next
two years (the Poor Rate books simply record "late Whitchurch" against
these years). But in July 1788, the three executors disposed of York
House to James Webber of Welbeck Street, Cavendish Square. The
following year the Twickenham and Syon Courts admitted Webber as
customary tenant for the copyhold lands. (The Syon Court charges were
moderate: 3s 6d in heriots and 3s 10d in fines; Twickenham Manor charges
were more severe: 7s 6½d in heriots and £36 in fines.) The total acreage,
freehold and copyhold, was nearly ten acres.

Webber also appeared in the Land Tax returns and the Poor Rate books from 1789 onwards but here he tended to be given his military rank, Major Webber (Lysons in 1810 refers to him as Lieutenant Colonel Webber). One new feature of the 1788 title deeds is the inclusion for the first time of the pews in St Mary's Church that appear to have gone with the ownership of York House since at least the Earl of Manchester's time. In 1788 these pews are recorded as pew 91 "in South Break" and pew 72 "in South Front Gallery above the stairs". This last was probably the servants' pew.

Of James Webber also, we know very little apart from his military rank and his London address. He still had an address in London when he came to sell the house in 1796. But his doing so caused Edward Ironside to add a hasty footnote to his *History and Antiquities of Twickenham*, then with the printers. For all its brevity it does suggest that Webber took an active interest in the House and was not an absentee landlord. Ironside's footnote reads quite simply as follows:

> "Lately in the occupation of Major James Webber who has at considerable expense greatly improved the house and grounds . . ."

THE AUSTRIAN AMBASSADOR AND HIS TWICKENHAM NEIGHBOURS

On 3 and 4 May 1796, James Webber by Indentures of Lease and Release transferred York House and its grounds to:

> "Louis Starhemberg a Count of the Holy Roman Empire Chamberlain to His Imperial Majesty and Minister Plenipotentiary to the Court of Great Britain and whose father was a natural born Subject of His Britannic Majesty".*

Stahremberg — the name was spelt variously — was the Austrian Ambassador. In due course he was admitted to the Syon Copyholds on 9 August 1796, having been admitted the day before to the Twickenham copyhold lands. The Count also appears in the Land Tax returns (but was marked as exempt, his name there being spelt "Stellingburg"), and was liable for the Twickenham Poor Rates (£5-10s in 1797). The Count was clearly

---

*MDR/1796/3/113. This claim to be a "British subject" (later deeds confer the status on the Count himself) was probably a polite legal fiction. See page 36 below.

pressed for ready money, for on 20 October 1798 the Syon Manor Court registered a £6000 mortgage against his name on his Twickenham property and, although this was cleared by April 1799, it was immediately replaced by a further mortgage of £5,500 which was not cleared for many years.* But then the Count had also to maintain a London house in Portland Square in addition to his Twickenham establishment.

Stahremberg had been born in Paris on 12 March 1762, the son of a prince with estates in Austria. His father was at this time the Austrian Ambassador to the French Court, which explains how Louis XV came to be the godfather to the child. Young Stahremberg in due course followed in his father's footsteps and became a diplomat, serving in Russia and then at the Hague. When the French invaded Holland in 1793, Stahremberg moved to London and became the Austrian (and Tuscan) representative here. By the time he bought York House he was thirty-four years old, married, and had a son and two daughters. He and his family were fond of music, opera, and amateur theatricals. For this last activity, he constructed a small theatre in York House sometime before 1801. He also had a private chapel in York House which, no doubt, enjoyed the customary diplomatic immunity.** As for the theatricals, he, his family, and members of his staff usually performed in short French plays, of which a number were staged between 1801 and 1805. The Count was clearly fond of Twickenham, but his family preferred London or Tunbridge. Stahremberg's duties also took him on occasion to Brighton to see the Prince of Wales. He was also absent on leave in Austria for the greater part of 1802; later still he was recalled to Vienna in 1807 after Austria had made peace with Napoleon. Whilst there he succeeded to his father's title and estates, as Prince Stahremberg. He served another tour in London from April 1809 to January 1810 whilst Austria was once more at war with France, but was recalled yet again when Austria made peace with Napoleon. He had a hatred of Napoleon, whose armies devastated his estates and added to his financial difficulties. He was also a marked man and had to travel at times on the Continent disguised as

*Not until 1821 according to the Syon Manor Court of 11 July 1821.

**In October 1804, the musician Giacomo Ferrari married the pianist, Miss Vittorina Henry, in the York House chapel (M. Hay, *Prince in Captivity,* p. 193).

a Jewish trader to avoid being arrested by the French. Although he continued to own York House after his departure in 1810, the Land Tax returns from 1810 onwards show his Twickenham property as "Late" Stahremberg.

Whilst he lived at York House, Stahremberg was frequently engaged in diplomatic activities. Laetitia Matilda Hawkins, who was at that time living in Sion Row, recalls seeing Stahremberg in earnest conversation with her neighbour the French royalist exile, the Comte de Jarnac. Stahremberg also entertained widely. For his amateur theatricals his guests included such persons as Mrs Anne Damer from Strawberry Hill, members of the British nobility, fellow Ambassadors, and the three Orleans princes (the Duc d'Orleans, the Duc de Montpensier, and the Comte de Beaujolais) then living at Highshot House in Crown Lane (now Crown Road). On one occasion the theatre was honoured with the presence of the Prince of Wales, the Duchess of Devonshire, and Mrs Fitzherbert up from Brighton.

The theatricals were sometimes accompanied by music; on other occasions the entertainment was purely musical. The Stahremberg daughters played and sang, as did the lovely Elizabeth Forbes, a visitor who spent the summers of 1805 and 1806 at Northend House opposite Montpelier Row. Stahremberg also brought down professionals — and friends — from London including Giacomo Gotifredo Ferrari and Domenico Dragonetti. There were also whist parties attended by one or other of the Orleans princes who also came to the musical evenings. Amongst the whist players was also the painter John Byrne "who is a very good whist player".*

This last comment appears in a letter written by the second of the Orleans princes, Antoine, Duc de Montpensier. He had lived with his two brothers in Twickenham since 1800. His letters for the years 1805-07 which describe the Twickenham scene were largely addressed to Mrs Forbes, the mother of Elizabeth, with whom he was in love but whom he

---

*This and other extracts from Montpensier's letters are from Malcolm Hay's *Prince in Captivity* (Eyre and Spottiswoode, 1960). The York House theatricals are dealt with in an article by Sybil Rosenfeld in the Twickenham Library. An account of the Orleans princes in Twickenham is to be found in BOTLHS Papers No. 32 and 49.

could not marry; royal protocol would not permit it. Mrs Forbes, when away from Twickenham, lived at Seaton in Scotland with her husband and her daughter. In Montpensier's letters there are other references to the Stahrembergs and their entertainments. In March 1806 Montpensier complains of too much hospitality: "between the Duke of Kent, and our good Stahr, I am always obliged to dine out, two or three times a week". Sometimes Montpensier refers to Stahremberg as "Stahr", sometimes he uses his nickname "Kukuk", who "likes our good old Twick and never "leaves it without regret". In July 1806 Montpensier notes the presence of the singer Ferrari at York House and adds, "I have been there pretty often". Later, after a trip to the country, he returns to Twickenham only to be "packed up in a carriage, for Castle-Hill [the Duke of Kent's house] where I found Stahr. All his ladies are at Tunbridge, but like a butterfly he flies continually from them to Town, and from Town to them. The next day we had him to dine with us [at Highshot House]." In December 1806, "Kukuk went to B [Brighton]." In the winter of 1806 Montpensier reports the arrival of a new Austrian diplomat at York House who had come to learn his trade from Stahremberg. This was the young Prince Esterhazy, "whose father is afflicted with a fortune of about one hundred thousand pounds a year". The young diplomat "seems good natured, open, unaffected, detesting the Corsican monster".

The Orleans princes found "Kukuk" good company, a generous host who shared their liking for "dear old Twick". A jovial soul also: "the old one was here this morning as mad and as cheerful as ever". The Stahrembergs were indeed "good and pleasant neighbours". Stahremberg, as already mentioned, was recalled to Vienna early in 1807. Montpensier's last reference to that family occurs in a letter of February 1807 when he writes, "The Stahrs . . . are going to Town *for good.*" This was the last time Montpensier was to see them, for they departed for Austria, whilst he, striken by consumption, died in May 1807.

York House remained empty for the next few years. There is a gap in the Land Tax records after 1810, but the next clue comes from the Poor Rate books of April 1812 and December 1813. These show that York House was now occupied by the Archbishop of Dublin, presumably as a tenant. By that date Stahremberg had left England for good (his last stay in London ended in January 1810). Richard Cobbett, writing in

1872, mentions the stay of the Archbishop of Dublin at York House, adding that Cleaver "from mental disease was unable to discharge the duties of the see". The Archbishop also had two very beautiful daughters and one of them married a Captain King R.N. in 1815. Whether this marriage took place from York House is not clear, but Cobbett mentions that in July 1817 the house is being advertised for sale. Archbishop Cleaver probably left York House late in 1816 since there are press reports of two social functions at the House in July 1816. He, at some date after that, moved to Tunbridge Wells where he died in December 1819 aged seventy-three.

Euseby Cleaver did not have a very distinguished career. He depended more on patronage than on talent. An Englishman, a parson's son, he went to Oxford and thereafter gained promotion through his brother, then a bishop, who had once been tutor to the Marquis of Buckingham. When that nobleman went out to Ireland as Viceroy, young Euseby Cleaver went as his chaplain. This was in 1787. By 1789 Cleaver was an Irish bishop and became Archbishop of Dublin in 1809. By 1811 or 1812, when he moved to York House, he was already mentally ill. But even in his saner days he had not been particularly active. His sole contribution to posterity seems to have been a sermon printed in 1792 on the need for Promoting English Protestant Schools in Ireland. The rest is silence.

The advertisement mentioned by Cobbett appeared in *The Times* on 3 July 1817 and contains little fresh information and a great deal of hyperbole:

> "The spacious FREEHOLD MANSION called York House, the property and late residence of Prince Stahremberg, most delightfully situate on the bank of the Thames, at Twickenham, with extensive attached and detached offices, coach-houses, stabling, conservatory, green-house, theatre, beautiful lawn and pleasure grounds in the highest order, capital kitchen-garden and meadow, the whole containing about 10 acres, partly freehold, the remainder copyhold of the manors of Isleworth Sion and Twickenham, and adapted for a family of the first distinction: also a cottage and garden in the occupation of Mr Cole."

This last would presumably be the house now called Langham Cottage.

As for Stahremberg, when *The Times* advertisement appeared, he had been out of England for seven years and was now Austrian Ambassador at Turin. But his monetary problems remained. His mortgage on York House was still outstanding, although it had passed through various hands and was now held by the Barings and a banker in Kent. York House, since Cleaver's departure, was empty, a drain on his purse. Worse still, in July 1817, a judgment went against him at the Court of Common Pleas in a Plea of Debt case. The Court found that Stahremberg owed the sum of £4186-12s-6d, which was chargeable against his property. When he — together with the Barings and the Kentish banker — managed to sell the house in September 1818, the sale raised only £3750.* The 1799 mortgage was not cleared in the Syon Manor Court until 1821. "Kukuk" meanwhile continued his diplomatic career on the Continent, dying in September 1833.

MRS DAMER AND THE JOHNSTONS (1818-1864)

Anne Seymour Damer was born in 1749, the daughter of Horace Walpole's close friend, Field Marshal Henry Seymour Conway and his wife, Lady Caroline Campbell. Anne was a great favourite of Horace Walpole, who praised her intellect and artistic talent to the skies. Her marriage, however, to the rich but shiftless John Damer proved disastrous. Running up vast debts, he shot himself. But Horace Walpole provided for Anne; when he died in 1797 she became executor of his Will and inherited Strawberry Hill (with money to keep it up) for life. She lived at Strawberry Hill until 1810 when she surrendered the estate and house to Lady Waldegrave.

Anne Damer did have artistic talent. Something of a blue stocking, she had studied in Italy and developed her skill as a sculptress. When she lived at Strawberry Hill, she had continued to sculpt and acquired a considerable reputation. She also staged there amateur theatricals including a play by one of the Miss Berrys. Mrs Damer was a radical whig in politics. She was acquainted with Josephine, Napoleon's first wife. When Joseph Farington, the artist and diarist, was in Paris during the short-lived Peace of Amiens, he visited the First Consul's apartments in the Tuilleries. In one of the rooms he noticed two busts by Mrs Damer, one of Charles James Fox and one of Lord Nelson. Farington did not think much of them, but then he was not a great admirer of Mrs Damer, whom he

*Map 2 shows the state of York House and its grounds at the time of the 1818 sale. The map is from the Middlesex Deeds Registry where it was entered in 1821 (MDR/1821/Bk 7/213).

30

thought knew little about painting, and he found "her manner and particularly her voice very affected and unpleasing".*

After giving up Strawberry Hill, Mrs Damer was sufficiently wealthy to maintain a fashionable house in London. Eventually she decided that she needed a house out of Town as well, and moved to Twickenham, possibly because her cousin, Mrs Lionel Damer, had moved there in 1816. Anne Damer purchased the vacant York House by a Deed dated 29 September 1818. A year later, in April and June 1819, the Manor Courts of Isleworth Syon and Twickenham formally transferred to her the copyhold lands of York House. The total cost to her of York House had been £3750, the copyhold lands alone costing £800 (equally divided between the two Manors).

Later historians, for instance Thorne writing in 1876, have recorded that once established in York House, Mrs Damer set up a studio there in what was subsequently to be the conservatory. But then both Cobbett (1872) and Thorne (1876) on no very sure grounds assert that she also frequently entertained Caroline of Brunswick, George IV's estranged wife, at York House. This is doubtful,** although Mrs Damer had befriended the Princess — who was also a sculptress — and remained loyal to her to the end. But Mrs Damer now divided her time between her London home in the winter and York House in the summer. It seems more likely that she saw most of her friends, such as Sarah Siddons, when in Town.

In the Poor Rate books and the Land Tax Returns, Mrs Damer appears both as owner and occupier of York House. The last entry against her name in the Poor Rate books is for May 1828. She died at her house in Upper Brook Street on 28 May 1828.

Farington Diary (1922 edition), Vol. 1, page 571, 5 June 1796.
**This tale is repeated by P. Noble, *Anne Seymour Damer* (1908), e.g. p. 214. Caroline, as Princess of Wales, had visited Strawberry Hill as Mrs Damer's guest in, for instance, 1809. Mrs Damer also visited the Princess in London. But by 1818 Mrs Damer was over 70 and not in good health and Caroline was out of the country. She did not return to England until the Spring of 1820, stood trial, and died in Augsut 1821. Mrs Damer did visit her in London and perhaps also in Brandenburgh House, Hammersmith, but did they ever meet in York House? A similar problem relates to Sarah Siddons, the actress and friend of Strawberry Hill days. Mrs Damer used to dine with her in London. But York House ?

Anne Damer's Will is a curious document. In making "Her much valued friend" Sir Jonathan Wathen Waller* her sole executor she added the condition that he should sell both York House and her leasehold estate in Upper Brook Street. After the payment of legacies the income from the residue was to go to her "cousin" Lady Johnston and after that lady's death it should be divided amongst her children. After making her Will in 1825, Mrs Damer added five codicils, which she did not hesitate to alter and amend subsequently in her own hand, and without the benefit of witnesses to those alterations or even an endorsement by herself. She left strict instructions as to her burial in her mother's tomb and set out the inscription that was to be added. Her coffin was to contain not only her "wallet" and chisels but also the bones of a favorite dog that were preserved in a box in her bedroom. She left generous legacies to her servants but struck their names out from the Will or the Codicils if they left her. She had a morbid fear of being buried alive and insisted in her Will that her executor should make absolutely sure that she was indeed dead. This was to be achieved either by first casting her corpse into a pit of quick lime, or it should be cut open before being placed in the coffin.

Cobbett, writing forty years afterwards, has it that Mrs Damer left York House to Lady Johnston. This seems to be a misapprehension. Mrs Damer did leave to her some family heirlooms, including a collection of her sculpted busts and terra cottas together with some worsted work of her mother's. But the Will laid down that York House should be sold. It was, in fact, acquired by Lady Johnston's husband by purchase. Sir Alexander Johnston bought the house for £6,500 of which £900 represented the notional value of the copyhold lands of the estate.

Sir Alexander Johnston (1775-1849) was an eminent lawyer. He had been brought up in Madras, where his father had an appointment with the Honorable East India Company. Johnston at an early age learnt to

*Waller had originally been Mr Phipps, the royal oculist. He changed his name and married Baroness Howe of Pope's Villa. Waller subsequently went blind. He had not originally been intended as Mrs Damer's executor but was added by a codicil after the death of her cousin, John Campbell, who would have been her chief beneficiary under the Will. Mrs Damer also removed the name of another executor, her man of business, though she left him a legacy of £500 so that he should not feel hurt.

speak Telegu, Tamil, and Hindustani. He subsequently read for the Bar at Lincoln's Inn and also studied for a time at Gottingen. Marrying in 1799 the daughter of Captain William Campbell R.N. (a cousin of Mrs Damer) he became successively Advocate General and Chief Justice of Ceylon, a territory captured from the Dutch and ceded to Britain at the Peace of Amiens.

Sir Alexander finally returned to Britain in 1819 and in retirement helped to found the Royal Asiatic Society in 1823. In 1832 he was made a Privy Councillor and was also involved in the establishment of the Judicial Committee of the Privy Council. He was a Liberal in politics and, for those times, interested in, and sympathetic towards, the native inhabitants of the Asian dependencies. When he came to Twickenham he was 56 years of age and had a family of four sons and three daughters. Walford, writing some thirty-four years after Johnston had died, records the story of the visit of the Brahmin and oriental scholar Raja Rammohan Roy* to York House as Johnston's guest. Cobbett, however, writing ten years earlier than Walford, makes no reference to the visit of this eminent Asian scholar.

Johnston also possessed a house and land in Scotland, and a house in London. It is difficult to be certain how much he used his home in Great Cumberland Place in preference to York House. Unfortunately the Poor Rate Books for much of that period have not survived. In those that do exist, Sir Alexander Johnston is listed in January and May 1845 as both owner and occupier, but in 1846 he is entered as "Sir Alexander Johnstone [sic] or occupier". The last Land Tax return extant for Twickenham is of a much earlier date; that for 1829, however, does show him as in occupation of his Twickenham property.

Cobbett, supported in part by evidence in the Poor Rate books, later suggested that York House was let out from time to time to tenants, possibly on short leases. One such tenant certainly was Mary, Dowager Duchess of Roxburghe. She had married the 4th Duke in 1789 and, after his death in 1805, she married in the following year John Tollemache (formerly John Manners) a son of Louisa Countess of Dysart (who owned Ham House). Tollemache died in York House on 13 February 1837. His

*Raja Rammoham Roy (1772-1833). A traveller, linguist, and writer of theological works.
**The Earldom had been revived in his favour. See *Complete Peerage.*

widow moved to Richmond, where she died, in 1838.

Another tenant mentioned by Cobbett was the Earl of Lonsdale. This was William Lowther (1757-1844) who had become Earl of Lonsdale in 1807.* His property and influence lay in Westmorland and he was a widower when he came to Twickenham. His exact dates of residence here are uncertain, but he would have been in his eighties when he came. What is certain is that he died in York House on 19 March 1844. Cobbett, writing 25 years later, and relying on local folk memory, states that Lonsdale was immensely popular in Twickenham, particularly with "the middle class inhabitants":

> "when his body was moved hence . . . nearly all the tradespeople followed in procession, some on foot and some on horseback, until it was out of the parish; and not a few travelled the whole way to Westmoreland."

The following year, when the Tithe Commission was at work in Twickenham, the York House lands are shown as owned by Sir Alexander Johnston but in the occupation of "Lord Lowther" (this was the usual courtesy title of the heir to the Lonsdale Earldom).

Thereafter there is uncertainty as to who, if any, occupied York House. The Johnstons appear to have been absent. The Censuses for 1841, 1851 and 1861 prove this. But Sir Alexander may have been in York House in 1845 and, more doubtfully, in 1846.

Johnston died at his London house on 6 March 1848. His widow, Lady Louisa, died at their home in Scotland in 1852. York House then passed to the four sons. Whilst, however, the eldest son, Lieutenant Colonel Thomas Henry Johnston, was admitted to the copyhold lands of the Twickenham manor, the youngest son, Frederick Erskine Johnston, was admitted to the Syon Manor copyhold lands because that manor followed the custom of "Borough English".**

*The Earldom had been revived in his favour. See *Complete Peerage.*

**For "Borough English" see page 3. Failure to make legal provision to overcome the custom of Borough English by surrendering the copyhold to one's Will in the Manor Court was a not uncommon error. For example a similar problem arose over parts of the Marble Hill estate upon the death of Lady Suffolk in 1767. The difficulty could be resolved by the customary heir immediately surrendering the copyhold to the heir named in the Will as was done in the Marble Hill case, but it did tend to complicate matters in the disposal of an estate by sale.

Cobbett suggests that York House was subsequently occupied — and eventually sold — by the Misses Johnston. The first statement may be correct. The surviving Poor Rate books for May and December 1855 and May and November 1856 show a "Miss Johnstone" as both owner and occupier. Her half yearly rates for 9 acres 2 roods and 2 perches of York House land came to £20-17s in May 1855. But in the light of later events it seems unlikely that Miss Johnston could have also owned the property, not least because two of her brothers had been admitted to the copyhold lands as the lawful heirs. Furthermore the stay of the Miss — or Misses — Johnston was clearly intermittent. Whilst the 1841 Census reveals that there were a number of servants in the house (Francis Deacon and his family, Mrs Webb and her children, and William Evans the coachman), the 1851 Census shows the house itself as empty with only William Webb, now aged 62, the gardener, living in the lodge.* As for the 1861 Census, the only resident in the house was Esther Doughley, aged 51, a housemaid. By 1863 the house was again vacant and ready for sale. But Cobbett is wrong in thinking that "the Misses Johnstone" sold it. The Conveyance Deeds of 1864 show that so far as the Johnstons were concerned it was the four brothers — Thomas Henry of the 6th Foot, Patrick Francis (now a general), Alexander Robert (living at Yoxford), and Frederick Erskine (Captain R.N.) — who were the vendors.

THE FRENCH CONNECTION

The sale of York House in 1864 was a complicated affair. In the first place, the four Johnston brothers had already had a sale by public auction in 1863, when the house and grounds, split into two lots, had been purchased by John Parsons for £7,000. But it would appear that the bulk of the money had not yet been paid. It seems that Parsons subsequently agreed with the Johnstons for a re-sale of the two lots, but at a better price. By the Conveyance of 11 March 1864 £8,600 was paid for York House and its grounds. The actual sum was divided as follows: £7,500 was

*Similarly the Voters' List for Twickenham Parish of 1853 has no entry for York House, although the other big houses of the Parish, such as Marble Hill, Fulwell Lodge, etc., are listed, either giving the names of the owners or (where property above a certain annual value was concerned) the occupiers.

for the freehold, of which Parsons got £1,600 and the Johnston brothers £5,900; £1,100 was for the copyhold (£900 for Twickenham Manor land and a mere £200 for Syon copyhold land). What is curious about the part that was Twickenham copyhold, and which was, of course, already part of the Johnston estate, was that most of the money seems to have been spent in recovering the eastern portion of Eel Pie Island, some two acres in extent. Nor was that all. A dispute over a tiny section called "The Swan's nest" at the downstream toe of the island had yet to be resolved. As a first move the new owners bought out the Lord of the Manor and the Twickenham copyhold was enfranchised by the payment of £695-14s-6d. The Swan's nest dispute was resolved in the following year by the purchase of the freehold of this tiny piece of land from the Lord of the Manor for £50.

The actual purchasers of the property were William Coulthurst and Hugh Antrobus, two of the directors of Coutts Bank in the Strand. In fact, they were a front for the real purchasers. Until the law was changed in 1870, aliens were not supposed to own real estate, although there was apparently little difficulty over tenancies or even leaseholds. In the past, Stahremberg had evaded this prohibition by claiming that he (or his father) were natural born subjects of His Britannic Majesty (the only known connection, and a weak one, was that Stahremberg's father had been the godson of George I — but this does not sound very convincing). More probably the lawyers were indulging in some polite legal fictions. But by 1864, the Coutts Directors and their clients were more concerned to observe the niceties. Behind the Directors, who were British subjects, was the Royal House of Orleans, for whom Coutts Bank had managed various matters since the 1780s. More recently the Directors had acted for the Duc d'Aumale in 1852 when they acquired Orleans House on his behalf and they were to act for him again in acquiring both Mount Lebanon and Riverside. In all probability, therefore, as the richest member of the family, Aumale put up the money for York House.

The actual occupant of the house was the young Comte de Paris, whose formal status was as a tenant holding a 21 year lease from Antrobus and Coulthurst, for which he paid £500 a year rent under the terms of the agreement of 21 July 1865. Louis Philippe Albert, Comte de Paris, had been born in 1838 when his grandfather, Louis Philippe, was King of the

French. Paris's father, Ferdinand Duc d'Orleans, had died in a carriage accident in 1842, leaving the boy as the immediate heir to the throne. But a Revolution broke out in February 1848. The old King abdicated in favour of his grandson. This proved useless and the whole family fled from France. King Louis Philippe settled at Claremont House in Esher where he died in 1850. Paris was now the Orleanist claimant to the French throne and regarded by his supporters as the rightful king, Philippe VII. Something of a scholar — he was to write a history of British Trade Unions — the Comte had served on the Staff of General George McClellan in the Army of the Potomac during the first year of the American Civil War (he later wrote a history of that conflict). In May 1864 he married his cousin, Marie Isabelle, at St Raphael's Catholic Church in Kingston.

Although the formal lease for York House was not made out until July 1865, the bride and groom took up residence in Twickenham in August 1864. Twickenham turned out en masse to greet them, and the streets were decked with bunting. A slight misunderstanding, whereby the crowds had gathered at the main gates only for the couple to enter by a side entrance, was diplomatically resolved by the Comte and his wife resuming their seats in the carriage and making a second, more formal, entry into the grounds of York House. There a reception committee of locals greeted them. The riverside meadow beyond the house was thrown open to over a thousand school children: each child received a fourpenny piece. The band of the 16th South West Middlesex Volunteers provided music. There were games and a Punch and Judy show. Finally, in the evening there was a firework display on Eel Pie Island with the centre piece displaying the words "WELCOME ROYAL GUESTS".

The Comte and Comtesse settled down to a busy life at York House for the next seven years. They did much entertaining and a good deal of social visiting. They were to be seen at Lady Waldegrave's fashionable gatherings at Strawberry Hill. In Desanges' painting of one such occasion in 1865, the Comte de Paris is shown in the Strawberry Hill drawing room, with a newspaper open in front of him, seated between the Countess of Clarendon and Lady John Russell and surrounded by other guests.

Paris also took an interest in local affairs. Whilst his uncle Aumale was the first — and life long — President of Twickenham Rowing Club, the Comte is credited with providing a slip of land on Eel Pie Island upon which the Club's present boathouse stands. As for York House, there is no clear evidence as to what alterations took place during Paris' occupation; possibly the saloon and winter garden were added (see the Annexe). Since he was technically a tenant of the Coutts Directors, he may have been limited in the extent to which he could undertake alterations. Certainly, he welcomed many visitors to the house when he was in residence. By chance, one of his Visitors' Books has survived. It is probably not the only book for the period 1864-71, nor does it record the endless visits of members of the Orleans family or close family friends. Also missing is the visit of Quarter Master Sergeant Louis Kyezor, a German Jew, who had settled at Whitton and had joined the South West Middlesex Volunteers. A man of spectacular inaccuracy on the rifle range, it was thought safer to make him QM and to allow him to design his own uniform. He is recorded as visiting the Comte on Volunteer business wearing a uniform "very like a general". When Kyezor was murdered at Whitton in October 1869, the Vicar of Whitton, in a letter to *The Times* described Kyezor as one of the best friends the Christians of Twickenham had ever had, adding that the Comte de Paris had "really loved the old man".

But to return to the Visitors' Book that has survived. It contains some fifty pages recording a wide range of visitors: more than one Vicar of St Mary's and the Vicar of Holy Trinity, Richard Cobbett the curate, ambassadors, politicians, inevitably French royalists, the Speaker of the House of Commons and his wife, Lady Dennison, on more than one occasion, the Marquis of Clanricarde, General and Lady Peel from Marble Hill, Monseigneur Weld, Field Marshal Blakeney, Vernon Harcourt M.P., General Cust, the Countess of Newburgh, the Rothschilds, Dean Stanley of Westminster, the Turkish Ambassador, and many others.

Whilst living at York House, three of the Comtesse's four children were born there: Marie Amelie in 1865, Louis Philippe Robert in 1869, and Helene in 1871. Shortly before this last child was born the Census of 1871 took place (the first census to find the house actually occupied by the owner and his family). Present on census day were the Comte and Comtesse, young Marie Amelie aged 5, Louis Philippe Duc d'Orleans aged 2, a Lady in Waiting, a visiting civil servant from Paris, a French army captain, 2 Ladies' maids, a cook, 3 nursery maids, 2 footmen, a valet, a second cook, 3 housemaids, a kitchen maid, 2 grooms, a gardener (Mark Needle) and his family. Most of the upper servants were French but two of the Nursery maids and the three housemaids were English.

The Household was on the verge of moving. War between France and Prussia had broken out in 1870. With the defeat of Napoleon III and the restoration of the French Republic, the Orleans princes were allowed back into France: one of them, Joinville, who had been living since 1866 at Mount Lebanon, was already back in France, fighting with the French army outside Orleans under an assumed name. By the end of 1871 all the French princes had left the neighbourhood. York House was to remain empty for some years.

The Comte de Paris and his wife did revisit Twickenham subsequently. They and their children and the Duchesse de Montpensier dined at York House as guests on 21 September 1881. When in 1884 the Comte de Paris and his family were again expelled from France, they settled for a time nearby, at Sheen House, Richmond. The Comte and Comtesse were present at the Consecration of St James' Church in Popes Grove by Cardinal Manning in 1887. In May 1889, the couple celebrated their silver wedding and Twickenham sent its compliments to Sheen House. Subsequently the Comtesse visited the Catholic schools in this parish and received an address of welcome at the Town Hall, then in King Street. Shortly afterwards, the Comte de Paris and his wife moved from Sheen House to Stowe in Buckinghamshire. There he died in 1894. His widow lived on until 1919.

The disposal of York House by Coulthurst and Antrobus was not without some difficulty. The sale of the house had been previewed by an article in *The Times* on 26 July 1873. The auction was set for 6 August. This turned out to be a flop. Thereafter a sale by private treaty was negotiated in February 1875 and the Comte de Paris made a formal surrender of his 21 year lease on 3 February 1875. The would-be purchaser was Captain W.J. Watson of the 8th Foot who agreed to pay £13,000 for York House. He put down an immediate deposit of £500. For several months thereafter the deal hung fire, although the lawyers acting for Antrobus and Coulthurst completed and engrossed — and had signed — the Conveyance. All that was required was for Watson to complete the payment but this he did not do. Eventually the sale was cancelled and the deposit was held in default. Even so, legal opinion had to be taken as to whether the completed but abortive conveyance blocked a future sale. Once this last hurdle was passed, Antrobus and Coulthurst, who had found another buyer, went ahead with a successful sale, but they had to accept a reduced price.

THE GRANT DUFFS

With the departure of the Comte de Paris and his family in 1871, York House remained empty for the next five years. During this time, the nominal owners, Coulthurst and Antrobus, secured the enfranchisement of the last remaining portion of copyhold land from the Duke of Northumberland as Lord of the Manor of Isleworth Syon: the fee was a modest £22. In addition they disposed of that corner of the York House estate on which Langham Cottage stood, together with its detached garden lying between the road and the riverside. The purchaser was the sitting tenant, George Augustus Powell, the sale taking place on 18 January 1872. Powell was a linen draper whose shop was in Church Street. His father, George, had been a Churchwarden with intermissions from 1846 until 1864.*

Finally, in October 1876, Antrobus and Coulthurst conveyed the now entirely freehold property of York House to Mountstuart Elphinstone Grant Duff. They had been compelled to drop the price, accepting £12,000 instead of the £13,000 they had hoped to get from Captain Watson a year previously. The map that accompanied the conveyance shows in some detail the state of the grounds and the extent of the buildings (Map 3).** It includes the ice house in the "Wilderness". However, a good deal of work was necessary by way of repairs and renovation before the new owner could move in with his family, which was towards the end of 1877.

Grant Duff was a Scot, a diminutive figure of a man — five feet four inches tall — shy, with a weak voice, and suffering from poor eye sight. He was also courageous. A politician, a Liberal M.P., he had already served as

*George Augustus Powell in his turn was also a Churchwarden, 1877-82.
**Note the tunnel under Sion Road which linked the grounds of York House and Mount Lebanon. It was later blocked up.

Under Secretary of State for India in Gladstone's first Ministry. He was also a man of wide literary tastes who entertained lavishly. At the time that he came to York House he was 49 years of age, married, and with a large and growing family which eventually numbered four sons and four daughters. Something of a scholar, a lover of animals and flowers, he was less patient with human beings. Accordingly to his eldest daughter (nick-named "Tiny") he could be extraordinarily brutal over self-satisfied stupidity, though kind to the genuinely ignorant. Despite his busy life and wide range of friends he spared time to help the small and struggling Twickenham Literary Society. Later he was a driving force behind the 1888 Bicentennial Exhibition in honour of Alexander Pope. Tiny's recollection of him was of a vital rather ugly red-bearded man who did not suffer little children too gladly. If he found any of his young ones in his wife's sitting room when he entered he was likely to dismiss them with a curt "Vanish, vanish".

Grant Duff was also a very clubable man who enjoyed discussions in male company, particularly on such topics as politics or literature. Although as a matter of form he attended the services of various denominations and entertained the clergy, he had little faith in any ortho-dox religion. His wife, who was a staunch supporter of St Mary's and of it social and welfare work, was nevertheless regarded by some members of her family as a complete agnostic.

A wide circle of friends came within Grant Duff's orbit and the visitors to York House were very numerous. His friendships took in most of the eminent men — and a few of the eminent women — of the day: Matthew Arnold, Palgrave, Disraeli, Jowett, John Morley, the Russells of Pembroke Lodge (including the young Bertrand who was Tiny's friend), Lady Walde-grave, Tennyson, Elizabeth Twining of Dial House, the Comte de Paris and his uncle Aumale, and many, many others. Karl Marx once dined with him at the Devonshire Club, Walter Pater and Sir Alfred Lyall stayed with him at York House. Laurence Oliphant, diplomat, writer, traveller and mystic died here during a visit in December 1888. Gladstone stayed at least twice (in May 1879 and July 1881). It was on one of these occasions, no doubt, that he took Tiny on his knee to kiss her: she did not like old gentlemen and was not amused. Dilke and his mistress (he later married her) also visited York House.

Much of his social life was recorded by Grant Duff in his diary, of which he later published 14 volumes under the title of *Notes from a Diary*. One of the best accounts of Grant Duff's days in Twickenham, however, is contained in Donald Simpson's *A Victorian Diarist at York House* and *Mrs Alford Remembers*.* From these accounts it appears that during the years 1877-1881, at York House alone, Grant Duff received some 670 visitors. After a gap — which will be touched on later — the number of visitors in years 1887-1891 totalled 1027. One of these visitors in the early years had been the Crown Princess of Germany** who was not only a friend of Grant Duff, but also the godmother to his daughter Victoria (known as "Dot").

Grant Duff's eldest daughter Tiny (she had been christened Clara Annabel Caroline)*** had a great friend, Maud Griffiths, whose family lived at Yelverton Lodge. Maud and Tiny were of the same age. In later years Maud Griffiths took on the task of reading to Grant Duff in his study in the mornings to save his failing eyes. It is probably this later period of the 1890s that Tiny had in mind when she described York House. By then it had five bathrooms. Her two small sisters slept in a large nursery with their nurse, their rooms being sparsely furnished, but the furnishings being of good quality. Tiny was given a free hand with her own room. The furniture was decorated in pale yellow with poppy designs (this was her mother's work). The guest rooms were very cheerful with Morris designs for the walls — daisies, cherries, plain blue, and one papered in salmon pink. But the house was still lighted by oil lamps, save on high occasions when there would be candles in the dining room.

Although the flower decorations were the work of Lady Grant Duff (Grant Duff was knighted in 1887), her husband also had an immense love of his flowers and his gardens. His diaries are full of references to them and to the various seasons — the yellow aconites, the croci, the flowering shrubs (particularly the lilac), the gentianella, the calceolarias (in his conservatory), the jasmin on the outer wall, the horse chestnut trees. He

*BOTLHS Papers No. 1 and No. 21.

**One such visit occurred in February 1879 and was reported in the *Richmond and Twickenham Times* on 22 February of that year.

***When small, 'Tiny' fell for a choir boy at St Mary's but never told him; he later became Sir Walter Alcock, organist of Salisbury Cathedral. Tiny also fell for Bertrand Russell's elder brother, Frank.

developed an interest in orchids and built an orchid house. He also made a hobby of collecting shells.

A final glimpse of the Grant Duff family towards the end of their first spell in York House comes with the Census of 1881. Present on that day were Grant Duff and his wife, three of his sons (Arthur aged 19, Evelyn 17, and Hampden 6),* three daughters (Tiny aged 10, Victoria 4, and Lily 4 months), his literary secretary Eunice Billaus (from Bengal), 6 visitors (two had brought ladies' maids with them) 15 servants, a groom and a nursery governess.

Mention was made earlier of a gap in the years in the Grant Duffs' stay at York House. It came about in this fashion. Grant Duff's political activities took him away from Twickenham often. He had a London House which he used a good deal, usually in the winter. He also travelled abroad frequently. In 1880 he abandoned York House for three months to the "sanitary engineers and contractors" (perhaps this marked the installation of the five bathrooms that Tiny remembered?). Then in 1881 he accepted the appointment of Governor of Madras. He left for India late in that same year and was absent from Twickenham until 1887. All the boys, save Hampden, the youngest, stayed in England, as did Victoria. Tiny was subsequently shipped home early from India in order to have some discipline instilled in her at Cheltenham Ladies College. Those children in England, and Lady Grant Duff on her periodic visits, appear to have used York House occasionally during these years, but more often than not stayed with relatives or lived in hired lodgings in London.

Although Grant Duff's term of office in Madras ended in 1886, he travelled for a while in the Levant and did not return to Twickenham until March of the following year. Thereafter the Visitors' books for 1887-91 are very full, but Grant Duff appears to have been away from Twickenham a great deal. Probably the last major family gathering at York House took place on 11 May 1895 when Tiny was married from the House. The bridegroom was Frederick Huth Jackson, the service was at St. Mary's, and Cosmo Gordon Lang (not yet a Bishop, let alone

---

*Presumably it was for his sons in the first instance that Grant Duff had a gymnasium built either in the house or in the grounds. The daughters came to enjoy boating and tennis with music in the evenings at York House. The boys, however, though they liked boating, did not like York House.

43

Archbishop) officiated.

A year later, in May 1896, Grant Duff let York House for one year to Mrs Blacker. He visited his old home once more in April 1897 prior to putting it up for sale. He himself lived on for another nine years, dying in his London home in January 1906.

THE FRENCH CONNECTION RENEWED

The new owner of York House had been born there on 6 February 1869. Louis Philippe Robert, Duc d'Orleans, was now, since the death of his father in 1894, the Pretender to the French throne and regarded by his followers as King Philippe VIII. He acquired York House on 8 May 1897 for the sum of £13,000. The Duc had recently married in 1896 the Archduchess Marie Dorothee of Austria. The couple were, however, to have no children.

Louis Philippe Robert did not move into York House immediately, but set about major alterations to the building. A local reporter some years later hazarded a guess that the Duc spent £40,000 on this work. Although this figure is almost certainly exaggerated there is no doubt that a considerable sum of money was spent. A new east wing was added (the portion that now contains the Large and Small Halls) to provide a museum for the Duc's hunting trophies acquired during a big game hunting trip to Africa during 1892-94. The wing also housed a swimming bath, sometimes referred to in the local press as a Turkish Bath. There were also new plumbing, drainage and sanitary installations. *The Builder* of December 1897 reported that the new drainage pipes totalled a mile in length and that electricity had been installed for several hundred lamps, for ventilating fans, and for an "electric launch". The electric fittings were designed in the style of the reigns of Louis XIV, XV and XVI, with the Orleans crest or coat of arms added as a further decoration. No doubt this theme influenced the exterior use of the fleur de lys which is still to be seen on brick panels and drain pipes. The Duc also had telephones installed but preserved "the oak Elizabethan staircase". New wrought iron gates with the Duc's coat of arms were erected at the entrance to the grounds and in the house there were new ceilings in "the Louis XV style". But the original "early Elizabethan style" ceiling of the first floor was retained. The whole house now had central heating, eighteen bedrooms for servants, modern baths, even towel airers. The floors were parquet but the entrance and conservatory floors were in black and white marble.* Externally a high brick wall in the grounds was erected to cut off the old river meadow from public view (this caused some local ill feeling and a petition of protest was lodged).

There were also fire appliances and hydrants. This last precaution was just as well since a fire broke out whilst workmen were still engaged in renovation work in October 1897. Flames and smoke were soon pouring from the roof close to one of the chimney stacks. The local Fire Brigade turned out, but before they had arrived the workmen had brought the blaze under control with "immense" volumes of water poured onto the burning roof. The cause of the outbreak was thought to be the overheating of a flue connected to two furnaces in the basement. Several old oak beams projected into that flue and had begun to smoulder and had eventually burst into flame.

Press reports suggested that the purchase of the house had been a wedding gift to the Duc by his great uncle, Aumale. The story was in circulation as early as December 1896, some months before the actual purchase was completed. It may well be true, since Aumale was not only the wealthiest member of the family, but had no children left to survive him. The last of his sons, the Duc de Guise, had died in Paris in 1872. What is more, when Aumale died in May 1897 he left his country house, Wood Norton near Evesham, to the Duc d'Orleans.

York House was ready for occupation by the end of 1897 and the Duc, his wife, and his hunting trophies moved in. These last included a stuffed elephant, lions, tigers, zebra, buck, crocodiles and flamingoes. No doubt the tigers came from the Duc's earlier visit to India when he had served as an officer in the 60th Rifles of the British Army. The Duc had been trained as a cadet at Sandhurst and had been commissioned, but had resigned his British commission in 1889. On reaching his 21st year he had crossed to France in an attempt to do his French military service, although his family were still exiled by law. This escapade led to his

*The Architects were Messrs Rogers Chapman & Thomas; the Contractors Messrs Leslie & Co; and the Engineers Messrs Rawlings Brothers. Since electricity did not come to Twickenham until 1902, York House would have had its own generator.

arrest and sentence of imprisonment for two years. He did not serve his sentence, being immediately pardoned and deported. As a consequence he won brief popularity and the title "The First Conscript of France". His next escapade caused a scandal: a too public affair with Nellie Melba, the singer. Her husband (known as "Kangaroo Charlie") at first was complaisant, but then started legal proceedings citing the Duc as co-respondent. Under pressure or payment the Duc's name was removed, whilst the Duc hastened off on his hunting safari to Africa. The death of his father, his marriage, and his residence in Twickenham were regarded as signs of his settling down after the sowing of wild oats. But the Duc's love of travel never left him, and in later years he became an explorer, particularly in the Arctic region. He was also an enthusiast for fast cars which he liked to drive himself.

It is difficult to say with any certainty how much time he and his wife spent at York House. Certainly they appear to have used Wood Norton a good deal, and the Duc's enthusiasm for building found a fresh outlet in the considerable alterations he undertook to his Wood Norton property.* Visits to Twickenham can only be placed with any certainty in the context of events that hit the newspaper columns. The couple were clearly present in October 1899 for the marriage of the Duc's youngest sister, Isabelle, to her cousin, Jean, son of the Duc de Chartres (on his marriage he was created Duc de Guise).

The religious ceremony took place at St Raphael's, Kingston, and the civil ceremony was at York House, Previously there had been a grand reception at Twickenham with some 250 guests. At the two functions, as well as a large contingent of French princes, and the widowed Comtesse de Paris, the great of the land were also present in force. Alexandra, Princess of Wales, and Princess Victoria represented the British Royal Family. In Twickenham crowds were out to greet the couple as they returned from Kingston and at St Mary's Church the bells rang out. Two local school children presented a bouquet and the town was generally en fete.

After the wedding the Duc paid another visit to Wood Norton and did not return to Twickenham until the middle of December 1899. He was

*He subsequently transferred his gates from York House to Wood Norton.

46

at Wood Norton once more in early January 1900 but came back to Twickenham by the 25th. This was in time for a reception on that day — a Thursday — for his royalist supporters. They came in great numbers; "almost every train from London in the afternoon brought visitors to York House". In the evening there was a large dinner party.

By now, however, the Duc had become unpopular locally. In part the walling in of the riverside meadow had aroused local feelings. The Duc was also now involved in a law suit concerning land on Eel Pie Island. His marriage was not a success* and local opinion may have sided with the Duchesse; perhaps because she liked York House and Twickenham. Fond of painting and sketching, she had her own studio in the house and filled it with her pictures. But the final blow was caused by the Duc's expression of pro-Boer sympathies in the Spring of 1900. In the process he was thought to have insulted the venerable Queen Victoria. Immediately he was dropped by his London Clubs and, worse still, reprimanded by the Editor of the *Richmond and Twickenham Times.** Wisely, the Duc took himself off to foreign parts for a while. Despite rumours in 1902, and subsequently, that he was about to return to York House, he did not do so, chosing in preference to use his Worcestershire residence. York House was put up for sale in 1903 but then withdrawn. In 1904, Orleans and his sister, Queen Marie Amelie of Portugal, visited York House, but this was for one day only. Almost certainly, this was the last visit that he paid to a house on which he had spent so much money and used so little. Finally in October 1906, York House was put up to auction by Messrs Chancellor. But three days earlier the *Richmond and Twickenham Times* reported that the house had already been sold to a Parsee merchant. The paper, if premature, was right.

*Eventually the couple separated. The Duchesse started a civil action for alimony in 1913 in the Brussels Civil Court.

**The paper removed his portrait from the front cover of their 1900 annual. Thereafter he was continually being taken to task for his actions. For example, "political reasons have led the head of the House to make himself unworthy of the name of gentleman by identifying himself with cowardly insults to the person of the most exalted and best-beloved lady in Europe". (*Richmond and Twickenham Times,* 7 April, 1900).

THE RATAN TATAS IN TWICKENHAM

The Duc d'Orleans sold York House for £16,000 to Ratanji Jamsetji Tata (better known to us as Sir Ratan Tata). Ratan Tata had been born in Bombay in 1871 and was educated at the Jesuit College of St. Xavier's. He was the younger of the two sons of Jamsetji Tata, the founder of the family business. Ratan Tata and his elder brother Dorabji Tata took charge of a large and growing business which included the Tata Steel Works. As these concerns prospered, so did the many charitable works of the family develop, including the Sir Ratan Tata Foundation in London with its support for the London School of Economics. Other charities in India also benefitted as did those in Twickenham. Sir Ratan subscribed generously; and the York House grounds were frequently made available for fetes and charity bazaars. Visitors in those early years included Baden Powell on Scouting business (in 1911)* and Gopal Krishna Gokhale, one time President of the Indian National Congress** (a visit still commemorated by the plaque in the York House grounds and "Gokhale Walk"). Although business took Ratan Tata back to India from time to time, when he was in Twickenham he preferred to live very quietly.

He and his wife, Navazbi Ratanji, spent a good deal of time in alterations to the interior of the house and to the grounds. As collectors of fine arts — paintings, china, glass, statuary, and other rare items — the couple used the house for a display of their collection. A press report of 1918 (written shortly after Sir Ratan's death) gives the following description of the house:

> "Not only was the interior largely rearranged, but a splendid French dining room was built on the site of what was known as the china room. This is a fine spacious apartment, lightly and delicately decorated and furnished, and containing two splendid pieces of Beauvais tapestry, as well as some Indian silver ware, exquisite specimens of craftsmanship."

*On 22 July, for a rally of Twickenham Scouts in York House grounds.

**Gokhale, on a visit to London, had suffered a heart attack and convalesced at York House during the spring and early summer of 1914. Another Indian leader whom Ratan Tata helped during these years was Gandhi who was in the middle of his passive resistance campaign in Natal, South Africa, aimed at improving the lot of Indians settled there. Tata was the first Indian to help finance Gandhi's movement. He did so on several occasions with substantial sums from November 1909.

48

As for the grounds:

> "The gardens too were altered, the walls running from the house to the riverside
> being erected and the sunk garden formed. About this time too, the Italian
> loggia on the north side of the house was built, and the famous statuary erected,
> while the beautiful rosary on the riverside of the road was made and the bridges
> across the road erected."

In fact, the first bridge — a wooden rustic affair — had been constructed
in the Duc d'Orleans' time around about 1898 (it was subsequently
demolished, within living memory). The stone bridge, which still survives,
was built in about 1911. The garden statues,* the sea nymphs and horses,
were acquired in 1909. Of Italian marble and in all probability carved in
Italy — or by Italian craftsmen — they originally stood in Lea Park near
Godalming, in the estate of the financier, Whitaker Wright, who killed
himself in 1904. His statuary was sold off. Some ended up in the possession of the Borough of Weston-super-Mare. Others, of a totally different
style, came to Twickenham. The arrival of one consignment proved
very eventful. On 23 June 1909 *The Thames Valley Times* carried a
report of an incident which occurred as the marble was being moved to
York House on Monday 21st June:

> "A large piece of Marble part of a huge statue, which has been secured from
> the late Mr Whittaker Wright's residence for erection in the grounds of York
> House, was being conveyed there on a trolley belonging to Mr James Vince
> when as it was turning the corner into Oak Lane, the Van overturned. The
> case containing the marble was thrown heavily to the ground and smashed,
> whilst the shafts of the cart were broken, and the horse which was thrown down,
> was slightly hurt. A portion of the hospital entrance gates was also knocked
> away. Luckily no one was near at the time, or the results might have been more
> serious. It was some hours before the marble was raised by means of a huge
> pulley and conveyed to its destination."

Even more remarkable, the report by its silence implies that the marble
was undamaged.

---

*Often referred to as the "Naiads", but these are the nymphs of rivers, streams, and
lakes. As the York House statues include giant sea horses and sea shells the nymphs
are more properly "Oceanides" (sea nymphs). The group has also been called "The
Birth of Venus" on account of the central female figure, or more briefly, "the Naked
Ladies". One possible candidate for this work is the Italian sculptor Marabitti (fl.
1904).

Tradition in the Singleton family (one of whose members had carried out specialised iron work at that time in the grounds of York House) has it that Sir Ratan Tata was not at first satisfied with the positioning of the statuary and had the pieces moved around from place to place in the grounds. Eventually he opted for the site that they now occupy in the riverside gardens of York House, which is where they were first placed.

Shortly after the purchase of York House, Sir Ratan Tata negotiated a mortgage of £10,000 on the house. Two points of interest arise from this transaction: the first being that the mortgagee was of unsound mind (the affair was handled by his legal guardians). Of more immediate interest, however, was the map of the estate which was attached to the deed (it is reproduced as Map 4). A comparison with the map of 1876 (Map 3) gives some idea of the changes both to the buildings and the grounds. The ice house, amongst other features, has disappeared.

By 1914, Sir Ratan Tata had paid off the mortgage on York House. In that same year, on the 9 July, a few weeks before the outbreak of War, Ratan Tata held one of those enormous "Edwardian" garden parties. Some 1500 guests came, the weather was "most felicitous", and the grounds charming. The local press managed to publish the names of some two hundred of the guests. Apart from the local M.P. Joynson-Hicks ("Jix") no Twickenham worthies were named. But the good and the great were out in force: the Maharaja of Baroda, the Earl and Countess of Mar, the Marquis of Downshire, the Earl of Dysart, General Sir Robert and Lady Baden-Powell (not on scouting business this time), Admiral Edmund Fremantle, Sir Alfred Mond, Granville Barker and his wife, the Greek Ambassador, T.P. O'Connor, Sir Moncherji Bhownagree. Sir Adolphus FitzGeorge, and many others. "Great interest was taken in the nearly completed armoury and extended museum". Two concerts, each an hour in duration, were performed in the museum. The band of the 5th Dragoon Guards played. "The whole of the house and grounds were open for inspection".

A month later, at 11 p.m. on 4 August, Britain was at War. After the outbreak of War, Ratan Tata returned to India. In July 1916 he became ill: it was decided that he must return to England for treatment. Whilst the S.S. *Arabia,* the ship on which he was travelling, was passing through the Mediterranean in November 1916, it was torpedoed and sunk.

Together with other survivors, Ratan Tata was in an open boat for some hours before being rescued. He was brought back to England and to York House,* but his health grew steadily worse. He was moved to St Ives in Cornwall, where he died on 5 September 1918.

The body was brought back to York House prior to the funeral at Brookwood cemetery. A large gathering was present: in addition to Lady Tata, there were representatives of the British and Indian Governments, members of the Parsee community, the Salvation Army, the University of London, and many relatives and friends. By his Will, Sir Ratan Tata left York House in trust to Lady Tata for her life.

Lady Tata lived on in York House for some years, but in 1922 decided to return to India. With the agreement of her Trustees, York House was put on the market. But first, Lady Tata decided to dispose of the great collection of antiques that she and her husband had collected and had displayed in York House. An auction lasting five days took place in the House and disposed of a wide range of collectors' items at prices which would today seem farcical (but then times have changed). Amongst the items were Japanese and Chinese curios, Venetian glass, 80 oil paintings (a Melloti for £190, a "reputed" Rubens for £47-10s, a Morland for £19), marble statuary (but not the riverside "Nymphs"),** motor cars, garden ornaments, a Wilton pile carpet (£46), a marble top table by Kent (£90), a Bechstein grand in a Sheraton design case (£200), a carved stone pagoda (£35), a Roman cistern (£50), a lead fountain (£50), a marble well head dated 1642 (£50), a life size Venus (£50), and many other items. The total sale raised £10,000. York House was once again empty and up for sale. But the House, which had in the past hundred years seen three

*A fellow passenger on that disastrous voyage was Dr Jivraji Mehta, who accompanied Sir Ratan Tata back to York House and stayed with him for a time. He had previously looked after G.K. Gokhale in the spring of 1914. Years later, when Indian High Commissioner in Britain, Dr. Mehta visited York House again.

**Interviewed in 1948, Miss Viner Brady said that her father in jest had claimed, as a conveyance fee from Lady Tata, the riverside statues, which he then gave to the Twickenham Council. It seems, however, that their sheer size discouraged anyone from buying them at the 1922 Auction, which preceded the sale of the house by two years. The Sea Nymphs had been offered for sale (Lot 785) on the fourth day of the Auction, but there were no takers.

families with close ties with India and the East, and had for so long been a family residence, had this time seen the last family depart. It was no longer to be a home.

AN END AND A NEW BEGINNING

At the very time that York House became vacant, the Twickenham Urban District Council was faced with a move from its existing premises in King Street on the termination of its lease. The Council had long been in possession of Radnor House, but this was not sufficiently central for its requirements. There was also on the market at this time Richmond House, lying between King Street and the River. Serious consideration was given to acquiring Richmond House and converting it to Council uses. Indeed, the Council went so far as to purchase the property. In the meantime, local opinion had become deeply divided on the issue and a tussle developed between the supporters of the Houses of Richmond and York.

A pressure group sprang up headed by Noel Viner Brady, Captain Alfred Burgess, Lt. Colonel Merrick and one or two others. In due course this informal group converted itself into the York House Society (active to this day) and proved very effective in rallying opinion — and the Councillors — in favour of York House.

A word must be said here about Noel Viner Brady, who was the driving force behind the group and acted behind the scenes as a negotiator with Estate Agents and Tata Trustees (the original asking price was £30,000), and as a lobbyist with Government Ministers (fortunately the local M.P. was one). Viner Brady was a solicitor by profession and had lived in Twickenham since about 1895. A Fellow of the Society of Antiquaries, and for a time a County Councillor on the Middlesex Council, he lived at "Ferryside". He remained active in local affairs to the end of his life.*

Under considerable pressure from local public opinion, the Twickenham Council finally agreed to purchase York House for use as the Council Offices. The eventual price agreed with the Tata Trustees was £20,500 and the conveyance was completed on 29th May 1924. To convert the house involved a further expenditure of £39,000 for alterations and new

---

*Viner Brady died in Twickenham in September 1945 aged 81. A plaque was unveiled in his memory at York House on 1 October 1948.

fittings. Loans were raised to meet this including two mortgages for £21,000 with the Prudential Assurance.* In the following year, 1925, the Council redeemed the Tithes due to the Vicar by way of a Rent Charge of £5-6s-5d by paying a lump sum of redemption money totalling £109-16s-6d to Queen Anne's Bounty.

In 1926 Twickenham received a Charter of Incorporation and became a municipal Borough. On 22 September the Charter bearing the Royal Seal was formally received at Richmond Bridge and escorted to York House. In the presence of many guests including Sir William Joynson-Hicks (now Home Secretary) and ex-King Manuel of Portugal** (now living at Fulwell Park), the Charter was received, blessed (by the Bishop of Willesden) and laid up in York House. The new Charter Mayor, the elderly Dr. J. Rudd Leeson,*** a long time resident of Twickenham, was present in his robes wearing his chain of office. This had been presented by the York House Society; the golden badge which went with it was the gift of the Twickenham Masonic Lodge and the Mayor's Mace was given by Dr Leeson himself.

The new Municipal Offices, however, were not formally opened until 16 November 1926 when the Duke and Duchess of York were present to perform the ceremony — probably the only royal Yorks ever to have visited York House. King Manuel was also there. His wife, Queen Augusta caused a stir: the press waxed lyrical over her magnificent sable coat. The Duke of York opened the new Council Chamber with a special key and later planted an oak sapling in the grounds. The Duchess won all hearts; not least little Rosemary and Michael Farrer, who, having presented her with a bouquet of flowers, kept coming back to stare up at her.

The following month, on 1st December, the York House Society held an inaugural ball under the patronage of King Manuel and Queen Augusta and Sir William and Lady Joynson-Hicks. Earlier the Society had presented to the Council a massive silver Loving Cup (dated 1732) to commemorate

*The Middlesex Council helped with a grant of up to £2093 for the maintenance of the grounds as public open spaces in perpetuity.

**King Manuel was the great, great grandson of Louis Philippe. His mother had been born in York House.

***Dr Leeson died a year later on 23 October 1927.

the acquisition of York House by the Borough.

* * * * * * * * *

York House has since then survived the enlargement of the Borough in
1937 (to take in Teddington and the Hamptons), bombing in the Second
World War, and the abolition of the short-lived Borough of Twickenham
in 1965. On the creation of the new and larger Borough of Richmond
upon Thames, the House became its headquarters.

There have, of course, been many changes. The old boathouse, opposite
Langham Cottage, has for years been leased out to the Twickenham Yacht
Club. A museum — to house exhibits donated by local councillors and
others — was opened in York House in the late 1920s on a voluntary basis,
but was closed by 1940 to make way for yet more offices (next to the
canteen). The liability of the House for the old Land Tax was redeemed
in 1950 by the Council by the payment of a sum of £7-9s-3d. In 1951,
York House was declared an "Ancient Monument" (curiously enough,
only part of the building, the oldest portion, is formally an "ancient
monument"; the rest is scheduled as a "listed building"). And in August
that same year, the electricity supply was switched from DC to AC!

Royal occasions, too, have played a part in recent times; as for instance
in late October 1951, when the flag on the roof of York House was
flown at half mast to mark the death of ex-Queen Marie Amelie of Portugal
(who had been born in the House in 1865). And for the Coronation of
Queen Elizabeth II in June 1953 the House was illuminated.

York House and its grounds have continued to be the subject of heated
local debate from time to time. In the autumn of 1955 the "old Dutch
Garden" was dug up to make way for a car park. This caused a considerable
public outcry against the destruction of what was thought to be an ancient
and unique garden (in point of fact the 1876 plan [Map 3] simply marks
the area as an "orchard garden"). Another local controversy arose in
1956 over the unveiling of a plaque at York House to commemorate
Edward Hyde, 1st Earl of Clarendon. A protracted argument followed in
the columns of the press as to whether Hyde had, or had not, ever lived
here. Shortly afterwards work was started on an extension to the office
buildings on the site flanking St Mary's Church. The cost was to be

£25,000, but in digging the foundations three ancient wells were uncovered. These were later filled in and the building was completed although there was belated opposition from the St Mary's Vicar and Churchwardens who took exception to the size and position of the building in proximity to the Church.

Yet another long running local dispute concerned the use to which the Champion's wharf site should be put. Champion's wharf, which adjoined the York House riverside gardens, had been purchased from the Church Authorities (principally the London Diocesan Board) for £22,500 at the end of March 1959. Preliminary plans for the site had included public lavatories and a tea shop. Eventually it was converted into the present day "Italian Terrace" just upstream of the Marble Statues.

These last have suffered from vandalism over the years; defaced, restored, and defaced again. The latest restoration, a major one costing a deal of money (in contrast to the face lift of September 1925 — a mere £96-10s), was supported by a public appeal, with a target of £55,000. A Trust was established by the York House Society and the Twickenham Society with generous help from the Council and the Tata Trustees. Work was completed in 1989. The Council, meanwhile, having built an imposing Civic Centre nearby in Arragon Road, has turned its attention to restoring and renovating York House. This work will take several years.

Once more the marble statues gleam and the fountains play in the gardens. When the work of renovation is complete, the old House can look forward with some confidence to the challenges of the new Century. After all, it has seen out four already.

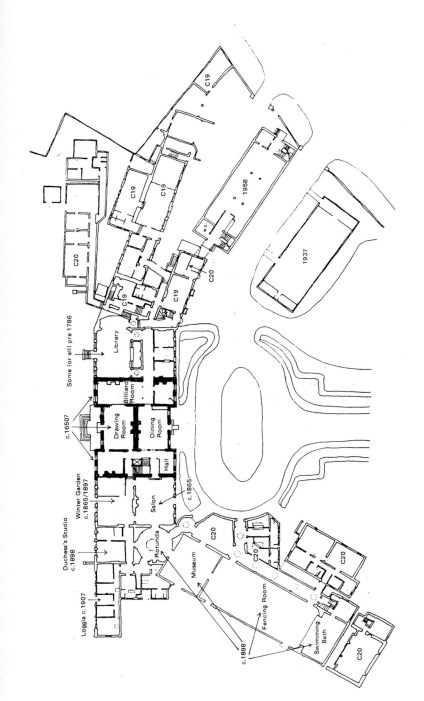

*Ground Floor plan of York House, showing approximate dates of
building and usage of main rooms c.1898*

Some (or all) pre 1786

Library

c.1650?

Drawing Room

Billiard Room

Dining Room

Hall

Salon

c.1865

Winter Garden c.1865/1897

Duchess's Studio c.1898

Loggia c.1907

Rotunda

Museum

C20

c.1898

Fencing Room

Swimming Bath

C20

C20

C20

C20

C19

C19

C19

C19

C19

C20

1937

1958

w.c.

ANNEXE

A preliminary note on the construction and later development of York House, by Anthony Beckles Willson

INTRODUCTORY

There is no clear-cut documentary evidence to give a date for the building of the original part of the house. What there is suggests that a house on the site was under construction as early as 1635 and that there has been a "Great" house on the land since before 1656. Further references allow the possibility that the present house was built between 1710 and 1719, but there is nothing positive to suggest that this is what actually happened.

The house has been so much extended, altered and refurbished that many of its original features have been removed or obscured, both inside and out. So a stylistic appraisal of the oldest fabric is not easy and only a thorough physical investigation could lead to a confident view about the age of the oldest parts.

Externally, the central building of three storeys, oriented exactly north-west/south-east, has all the basic attributes of a substantial house dating from the 17th Century or even the early years of the 18th Century. This central portion, originally with or without wings, is seven windows wide with a recessed centre section three windows wide. The roof is, today, covered with ungraduated slates and has a steep pitch of about 45°. There are cellars beneath the whole of the house. This part of the house is recognisable in the earliest known complete representation of it; a water colour of the Twickenham riverside by Edward Ironside dated 1786. A later view, an engraving by James Peller Malcolm, made c.1808, shows what is clearly the same house, but in greater detail. Both these views show wings at each end of the central block; and roof alterations which, as explained below, were made after the house was first built.

THE EXTERIOR

As seen today, the red brick walls are faced in Flemish bond, which was introduced to England early in the 17th Century and by its end had largely superseded English bond.*

The bricks used for the centre section of the front facade seem more regular than those on the bays, possibly because this section has been tuck-pointed. There are also areas of tuck-pointing remaining on each flank of the building, though none on the garden front. The bricks on the bays at the front, pointed at present with coloured mortar and finished with a bagged joint, are fairly rough in texture. The general effect which this creates seems more comfortable than the tuck-pointing.**

There is a slight difference of quality between the brickwork to the centre section on the garden side and that of the flanking bays.

There is a central chimney stack which, today, sports no less than eleven flues. A view of 1898 shows the same number. It is hard, superficially, to account for such a number of fireplaces on three floors of the centre of the building. The original plan suggests the possibility of up to six, and while there may have been fireplaces in the cellars originally, they cannot at present be seen.

The window heads are flat, formed of cut and/or rubbed (gauged) red bricks, four courses high, a technique probably introduced from Holland around 1630 (see Kew Palace, 1631, for an early example). They have stucco "keystones", which have been applied over the brickwork. These look fussy and were possibly added when the house was extensively worked over for one of the French occupations, after 1865 or 1897.

The external angles of each of the outer bays are dressed with rusticated stucco to simulate stone, each "stone" four courses high and chamfered. The colour is slightly different from the ground floor. The whole of the ground storey is rendered to simulate rusticated stone, with recessed square coursing, and on the front facade this extends across the flanking wings. The rendering seems all of a piece, suggesting that it was either applied or completely renewed much later than the original building. On the garden side the rendering is confined to the main original block, but overlaps slightly the brickwork of the two flanking wings. This

---

*The parish church next door, rebuilt in 1715 under the direction of John James, employs English bond still.

**Tuck-pointing was introduced to England during the 18th Century, that to Twickenham parish church being an early example.

58

implies that, in its present form at least, it post-dates the wings. Investigation might show what originally lay beneath.

The centre sections of both front and garden facades have natural limestone plinths about 18 inches high. It seems likely, from this survival, that the ground floor was originally of facing brick and it is possible that this was itself rusticated. Malcolm's engraving of 1808 shows ground floor stone or stucco but none on the upper quoins. Ironside's watercolour of 1786 shows what appears to be stonework or stucco to the ground floor of the centre section of the garden front, but nothing on the outer bays.

The whole of the roof over the second floor of the garden front has been raised at some stage after the house was built. This alteration, shown on Ironside's watercolour of 1786, can be seen today within the roof space, where some of the original timbering is still in place. The carpentry of the altered roof structure is not well conceived, as though the design had not been properly thought out before the work was attempted. The intention seems to have been to "improve" the house by making it look more important, but it has not done it any good: the junction of the large centre hip with the outer bays is plain awkward, particularly as it is recessed. The outer pairs of windows have been raised in height too, though this could have been at a later date, when the gallery was subdivided (see below). The effect is to leave the three centre windows with a disproportionate height of brickwork over them.

The face of the south-west bay on the garden facade steps forward eight inches for a large part of its width. This gives much of the bay a greater projection than its pair. The roof has been adjusted to accommodate this so either the step pre-dates the roof raising or the roof was rebuilt, again, when the step was added. The reason for this long-standing feature is not readily explainable. However, the two horizontal steel straps at high level are evidence of structural movement in this part of the building, possibly due to some ground condition and the difference of plane may represent an additional whole brick skin added in an attempt to strengthen the wall. It has been there at least as long as the adjoining wing which has been built flush with it, so the alteration may have been made before 1786.

Most of the present windows are inward opening casements which, together with the shutters, were possibly inserted as part of the extensive refurbishment by the Duc d'Orleans in 1897/98 when he bought the property. The casements replaced the sash windows shown in 1808.*

ADDITIONS TO THE HOUSE

The wing buildings mentioned earlier may have existed or been added, in various forms, from the very beginning. Clarendon was assessed for 37 hearths in 1664 and 43 hearths in 1666. The main house looks as though it had originally not more than about 18 fireplaces at ground level and above. Of the balance of up to 25 hearths, some might have been in the cellars, but others would have been in the staff quarters and ancillary accommodation, some of which might have abutted the main block.

By 1742 substantial additions are noted, and single storey wings are shown on the view of 1786. By c.1808 the south-west wing appears to have a set-back clerestorey of five windows, the centre one being semi-circular, and the north-east wing is nearly three storeys high. Both wings have ground floor windows opening on to the garden.

Some of this work may have been continued by Count Stahremberg, who bought the house in 1796, and by 1801 had constructed a small theatre, and chapel there.

A map dated 1821 (Memorial in Middlesex Deeds Registry of the 1818 Conveyance MDR/1821/7/213) gives a plan of the house and grounds as bought by Mrs Anne Damer. The south-west wing is drawn and described as a complex of "offices" apparently around a courtyard (Map 2).

The north-east wing is shown with a single "office" at the front, and a long "greenhouse" on the garden side. The extent of the "greenhouse" approximates to the length, today, of the Winter Garden cum Conservatory (now canteen) and its present day extension, the "Duchess's Studio", so described in the sale particulars for 1903 and 1906.

This single storey extension, decorated with the obligatory fleur-de-lys outside, was built by the Duc d'Orleans for his new Duchess c. 1898. She was a keen amateur artist.

Beyond this is the Italian Loggia. It has been suggested that the five sculptural plaques built into upper parts of the walls of the Loggia might

---

*These would certainly have replaced original casement windows which would have been usual before the first use of sash windows in England c.1676.

be the work of Anne Damer. This seems unlikely, unless they were moved from another part of the house, because the Loggia was not built until after Sir Ratan Tata bought the house in 1906.

The room today known as the Salon is not shown on the map for 1821, nor on Warren's tithe map of 1846, nor on the 25 inch Ordnance Survey map of 1864. It is probably a part of the building by 1873 and was possibly built by the Comte de Paris, although it is then described differently:

"A handsome Dining Room. 33' by 25'; 13'6" high . . . lighted by 7 windows . . ." (in fact the salon today only has five windows. A photograph of this room of c.1897 shows a sixth window where there is now the doorway into the octagonal room beyond).

This was a fair way from the kitchens, assumed to have been, throughout the life of the house, at ground floor level. By the time of the sale by the Duc d'Orleans in 1906 it had become "The Drawing Room"; the dining room had moved over to the present Entrance Hall and the present Large Committee Room was described as "The Salon". This room had a wide opening leading to the Billiard Room, now the Mayor's Parlour.

The largest single extension to the house was "The Grand Museum", connected by stairs to "The Swimming bath", to which was attached a "Turkish Bath, entirely lined with marble". All this, today, is the large Hall used for public functions.

THE INTERIOR

The interior of the house has been much altered in appearance and finish by successive waves of refurbishment and in places suffers grievously from the result of 60 years adventitious use as Local Government offices. Much of the work carried out for the two French occupations remains — the use of the fleur-de-lys is widespread, on door handles, fire-backs and worked into plasterwork and decoration. Even the wire balloons to the tops of vent pipes at roof level have fleur-de-lys on them. However, there are a number of handsome fireplaces, much elegant plasterwork and timber panelling, a great deal of which predates this period. Some elements date from the 18th Century and one ceiling in particular, to the centre room at first floor level on the garden side, may belong to the 17th Century.

61

Part of the decoration in the field of this ceiling depicts birds: muscovy ducks or conceivably herons, or even shags; no doubt an allusion to the nearby river.

The windows mentioned above in connection with the roof-raising originally served what was, in 1742, ". . . a large Gallery of 70 Feet, stucco'd . . .". Later the gallery was sub-divided to provide four separate rooms. There is nothing to show at present if the subdivision of the gallery is contemporary with the roof alterations, or even when the windows were altered. Most of the original, continuous, corniced ceiling remains, the only missing section is in the south-west room where a new ceiling has been inserted at a lower level. Vestiges of the original ceiling are visible above in the roof-space.

The ceiling to the long gallery, with its generous cove, is similar in form to four other ceilings covering most of this floor. One, with somewhat more ornate plasterwork, is over the staircase and, although heavily redecorated, it does not appear to be of modern construction. It matches the well of the staircase and is clearly stylistically of a piece with the staircase which has been generally accepted to be of mid-17th Century design. If one accepts this, assuming that the staircase was built specifically for the house, then the ceiling pattern for the whole of the second floor can be taken to be of a similar period, which effectively dates the house to around 1650.

It is also apparent that the second floor of this house was originally part of the owner's own accommodation — it did not house attics for staff; this alone suggests that there was always a considerable amount of ancillary accommodation elsewhere on the estate, some of it presumably attached to the house.

The cellars today are much obscured by storage and racking, and only some are accessible. The room beneath the south-west bay on the garden side has a fairly ancient door frame and has been lowered by 18 inches. Generally the cellars have stone flagged floors, and some have been tiled with white square edged tiles indicating earlier use for catering storage.

ROOF CONSTRUCTION

The timbering in the roof bears witness to successive waves of repair and alteration. Some of this is of fairly jobbing quality. Much of the original oak timbering survives, whether it still performs any useful function or not. On the garden side it has been used as a means of support for the raised roof structure, carried out in pine, rather than oak. On the north-east flank there has been wholesale repair work in pine, but much of the old work has been left. The central section of the roof is modern, and has involved the infilling, to ridge level all round, of the valley through which the centre stack of chimneys rises. This involved the removal of the inner halves of all of the original roof trusses, purlins and their rafters over the centre bay of the house.

Some of the original trusses carry sequential numbers identifying their intended position in the roof at the time of erection.

CONCLUSION

So far very little work has been undertaken at York House to catalogue or record its features and their history. Much could be done that could lead to an invaluable chronology of the various alterations to the original house and its extensions. Such an enterprise would perhaps start with a proper measured survey, continue with a study, employing systematic photography of the fabric (fireplaces, plasterwork, panelling, staircase, roof timbers, cellars, etc.), and perhaps culminate with an attribution for the sculptor of the bas-relief plaques built into the Italian loggia walls.

Note: *This is a summary of a longer and much more detailed report (together with photographs) prepared in January 1990.*

CHRONOLOGY

Date	Owner		Tenant	
1633			Andrew Pitcarne	Acquires leases of York Farm
1635				Moses Glover map shows scaffolding
Feb 1637	Andrew Pitcarne	d.1640		Obtains freehold 1637
Nov 1640	Widow Pitcarne	d.1653		
1653	Son, Charles Pitcarne			
1656	Earl of Manchester			Described in 1661 as "his Great House" It is the largest in Twickenham
1661	Earl of Clarendon	d.1674		In exile from 1667
1668/84			Countess of Anglesey Lord Arundell Lady Falmouth	
Dec 1674	Laurence Hyde			Inherits house
Apr 1689	Sir Charles Tufton	d.1708		
May 1708	Widow Tufton	d.1719/20		
Jul 1710				House for sale: "It was the Lord Chancellor's"
1720	Thomas Vernon	d.1726	Hon. Richard Edgcumbe Dowager Lady Exeter Duke of Rutland	
1727	Widow Jane Vernon			
c.1734	Eliz. & Pawlett St John			
Apr 1738	Joshua Naylor			
Jul 1746	James Whitchurch	d.1785/86		Today's house recognisable from Ironside's description Ironside view: single storey wings shown and roof raised
1786				

Date	Occupant	Occupant	(died)	Event
Jul 1789	Lt Col James Webber			Makes alterations to house
May 1796	Count Stahremberg			Constructs theatre & chapel
c.1808				Garden front view by J P Malcolm shows wings rebuilt
1812/16		Archbishop Cleaver		
Sep 1818	Mrs Anne Seymour Damer		d.1828	Sculpts in conservatory
Sep 1828	Sir Alexander Johnston		d.1849	
?/1837		Duchess of Roxburghe	d.1838	
1828/44		Earl of Lonsdale	d.1844	
1849	Sons of Johnston			
Mar 1864	Coutts Bank Directors			
Aug 1864		Comte de Paris		Salon and Winter Garden built?
				Windows altered?
Sep 1873				House empty
Oct 1876	Sir M E Grant Duff			Substantial refurbishment undertaken
				Builds gymnasium for children
Aug 1879				Storm wrecks Greenhouse and Conservatory
				much damage to house
Feb 1880				Sanitary Engineers and Contractors at work
1880/86				House empty
Nov 1889				Orchid House opened
1896/97		Mrs Blacker		
May 1897	Duc d'Orleans			House refurbished. Museum/Pool built
				Winter Garden/Conservatory built?
				Duchess's Studio built
1900				House empty
Dec 1906	Sir Ratan Tata		d.1918	Italian Loggia built, with sculpture
	Lady Tata			
1922				House empty
1924	Twickenham UDC			House altered for use as offices

SELECT BIBLIOGRAPHY
(Note: a fully annotated copy of this paper has been deposited at the
Twickenham Reference Library)

Public Record Office
E/178/4499 (Special Commissions, Middlesex, 1637)
C 54/4086 membranes 36-37 (1661 Deed)
PROB/11 (Wills) — 11/184 (Andrew Pitcarne); 11/501 (Sir Charles
Tufton); 11/574 (Dame Ayliffe Tufton); 11/1139 (James Whitchurch);
11/1741 (Anne Seymour Damer)

The Corporation of London Greater London Record Office
ACC/543 (1689 Indentures for York Farm and Twickenham Manor)
ACC/1379 (Syon Manor Court books)
ACC 782 (Twickenham Manor Court books)
MR/LPT/1597-1634 (Twickenham Land Tax returns 1767, 1780-1829)
MDR (Middlesex Deeds Registry 1709-1938)
ACC 1789 (Papers relating to York House 1865-1903)

Twickenham Reference Library
Censuses, Twickenham 1841, 1851, 1861, 1871 (1881 at Richmond
Reference Library)
Twickenham Poor Rate Books (incomplete) 1748-1865; also Highways
Rates Books
Twickenham Enclosure Award 1818
Council Minutes; also Volume "Management and Development
Committee minutes 1924-26"
York House Vertical Files, and Albums of Photographs
York House Sale catalogues, 1903, 1906, 1922
Book of Twickenham (Collection of Documents)
Sybil Rosenfeld: Typescript articles — "Theatricals at York House",
". . . Theatricals at Strawberry Hill"
Miscellaneous Documents (originals & photocopies) including L347:
94T (1741, Vernon case for legal opinion); Doc. 470 (1656) Indenture
between Charles Pitcarne & others

Municipal Offices, York House
York House Title Deeds, files TD/11 and TD/11A (1828 to the present)

St Mary's Church
Church Wardens' Accounts
Vestry Minutes
Poor Rates Book 1663-1672
Tithe Award 1845
Registers of baptisms, marriages, and burials

Simpson Papers
Correspondence and cuttings relating to York House, etc.

BOOKS AND ARTICLES

A. Tilney Bassett, ed. (introduction by Mrs Huth Jackson) — *A Victorian Vintage* (1930)

Bishop Burnet — *The History of his own Times* (Everyman edition, 1922)

Stella Campbell — *The Hyde Family and York House, Twickenham* (Middlesex Local History Council Bulletin No. 6, 1958)

Calendar of State Papers, Domestic

R. Cobbett — *Memorials of Twickenham* (1872)

The Complete Peerage

B. Cox — *Wood Norton* (Vale of Evesham Historical Society, 1975)

Dictionary of National Biography

A. Fremantle — *Three Cornered Heart* (Curtis, New York 1970 edition)

Malcolm Hay — *Prince in Captivity* (1960)

Gervas Huxley — *Endymion Porter* (1959)

Donald W. Insall — *A Study of York House and its Gardens . . .* (July 1988 — for the Borough of Richmond upon Thames)

E. Ironside — *History and Antiquities of Twickenham* (1797)

Annabel Huth Jackson — *A Victorian Childhood* (1932)

J.H. Jesse — *History of the Court of England during the Reign of the Stuarts* (1846)

J.H. Jesse — *Memoirs of the Court in England from the Revolution of 1688 . . .* (1846)

Lady T. Lewis — *Journals of the Misses Berry* (1866)

W.S. Lewis, ed. — *Walpole's Correspondence*

T.H. Lister — *Life and Administration of Edward 1st Earl of Clarendon* (1837)

D. Lysons — *Environs of London* (1810 edition)

P. Noble — *Anne Seymour Damer* (1908)

R. Ollard — *Clarendon and his Friends* (1989)

Pepys Diary (Wheatley Edition 1928)

C. Pitcairn — *History of the Fife Pitcairns* (1905)

R. Pocock — *Memorials of the Tufton Family* (1800)

F.J. Routledge, ed. — *Calendar of the Clarendon State Papers*, Vol. 5 (1970)

D.N. Smith, ed. — *Characters from the Histories and Memoirs of the 17th Century* (1920)

J. Thorne — *Handbook to the Environs of London* (1876)

Twickenham Council — *Commemorative booklet, Charter Day* (1926)

Official Handbook (1947)

Official Guide, York House (editions 1927-1939)

Victoria County History, Middlesex, Vol. 3 (1962)

E. Walford — *Greater London* (1883/4)

Newspapers:

The Surrey Comet, The Richmond and Twickenham Times, Thames Valley Times, The Builder, The Gentleman's Magazine, and *The Times*

Borough of Twickenham Local History Society Papers

No. 1: *A Victorian Diarist at York House*

No. 21: *Mrs Alford Remembers — Twickenham in the 1880s*

No. 32: *Highshot House*

No. 35: *Twickenham Society in Queen Anne's Reign*

No. 49: *The Orleans Family in Twickenham*

No. 60: *The Manor House, Twickenham*

Library Notes

No. 3: on Local History "York House, Twickenham" (several editions)

ACKNOWLEDGEMENTS

I wish to thank the following for permission to use or reproduce material
in this paper: the Controller of Her Majesty's Stationery Office for Crown
Copyright material; the Keeper of the Public Record Office for other
material in the PRO; Richard Ollard and the Oxford University Press for
quotations from *Clarendon and his Friends;* Messrs Eyre and Spottiswoode
for extracts from Montpensier's letters in *Prince in Captivity* by the late
Dr Malcolm Hay; the Corporation of London: Greater London Record
Office for material quoted from the GLRO Archives and for permission
to reproduce two plans of the York House Estate from the Middlesex
Deeds Registry; Sybil Rosenfeld for the use of her two typescript articles
on Theatricals at York House and at Strawberry Hill; the Vicar and
Churchwardens of St Mary's Twickenham for permission to see certain
original documents (microfiche copies of much of the Parish Records,
together with certain transcripts, are to be found in Twickenham Library);
His Grace the Duke of Northumberland for a detail of Glover's map; and
the London Borough of Richmond upon Thames for the estate plan of
1907 from the York House Title deeds. The balance of illustrations are
drawn from the collection in the Twickenham Library save for Figures
8-11 and 15 which are from Donald Simpson's own collection of prints
and photographs. The modern photographs of York House are by Alan
Urwin. Again my grateful thanks.

Many individual have helped in making this paper possible and deserve a
personal note of thanks. These include the Staffs of the PRO, the GLRO,
the Guildhall Library, and Twickenham and Richmond Libraries, and
more especially Diana Howard, Derek Jones, Jane Baxter and Brian Reid;
and also W. & A. Houben, Bridget Howlett, Jennifer Mills (who gave me
her own notes on York House), Ted Rothery and Robert Ellis at York
House, Elizabeth Dumbell, Elsie Rowlands, Joan Heath, John Hart, Ted
Morris, Patricia Simpson, the Society's Publication Committee (who kept
me up to the mark), Tony Beckles Willson (for the Annexe and for guiding
an idiot more or less unharmed through some minefields), and last, but
far from least, Donald Simpson and Alan Urwin for their patience and
help. Those whom I may have forgotten must accept my intended thanks
and my deep apologies.